Praise for *Mentorship Matters: Now More than Ever!*

"Mentorship Matters is an extremely useful and structured discussion and understanding of modern mentorship. It makes use of history-based storytelling and case studies that reveal the anatomy of what an effective mentoring program looks like. As institutions evolve from Servant Leadership to Leadership as a Service (LaaS) it's clear that mentoring will be a key source of value creation for tomorrow's leaders developing tomorrow's leaders."

– Russ Klein, CEO, American Marketing Association

"Craig Lund and David Kincaid, my standing ovation for having a dream and then acting on it and Alan Middleton, an educator of the highest level, for writing this book. Mentoring is a series of moments and exchanges of gifts that last a lifetime. This book is living proof of the value of this time well spent. Inside are magical stories of YODA's, the mentors who invested their time to inspire, educate, share and motivate and also to listen and learn, and the people who dared to raise their hand go on a quest of discovery and enlightenment with a stranger, who will morph into a trusted confidant."

– Tony Chapman, Host of *Chatter that Matters*

"Having been a mentor in the Mentor Exchange program, I can attest to the value gained being a mentor. Craig & David have worked tirelessly to connect ambitious young professionals with experienced Mentors creating productive relationships that will last a lifetime."

– Paul Rowan – Co-Founder of Umbra

D09986200

MENTORSHIP MATTERS

MATTERS

Now More than Ever!

MENTORSHIP MATTERS

Now More than Ever!

Alan C. Middleton PhD

Copyright © Alan C. Middleton.

First edition, 2021

Publisher: American Marketing Association, Toronto Chapter

Cover & interior layout design by Andy Meaden meadencreative.com

Copy Editor: Barry Lyons

Proof-reader: Miglena Nikolova

Middleton, Alan. C. Mentorship Matters: Now More than Ever! / Alan C. Middleton, PhD

p. cm. Originally published with sponsorship of American Marketing Association Toronto Chapter, 2021.

ISBN Paperback 978-1-7778066-0-6

ISBN eBook 978-1-7778066-1-3

CONTENTS

FOREWORD

For more than 10 years we've been honoured to serve as co-chairs of AMA Toronto's Mentor Exchange.

The Exchange brought together its first successful pairing of a mentor and mentee in 2010. Since then, we've learned an enormous amount about the nature and purpose of mentorship. We've also re-evaluated and refined our ideas about mentorship, discarding along the way some of the common misconceptions that many of us hold before we become either a mentor or a mentee. For example:

- Mentorship is not a process; it's a capability. Whether you're a mentor or a mentee, the relationship challenges you in ways you might not expect. In addressing those challenges, you inevitably draw on resources that you may not previously have recognized in yourself.

- Mentorship is not just a title. It's a fundamentally personal interaction. It brings together two people based on their needs and skills, who challenge each other to grow in rewarding and sometimes unexpected ways.

- Mentorship is not a program. When you join the Mentor Exchange as a mentor or mentee, you're signing up for a deep and lasting relationship. As we've discovered in our own experience, that relationship may continue long after the formal one-year term has come to an end. In our case, both of us have maintained contact with almost all of the mentees with whom we've worked since 2010.

So, if mentorship is not a process, a title, or a program, what is it?

- Mentorship draws on the leadership capabilities of both parties. Individuals become involved in the Mentor Exchange because they want to illuminate, define, apply, and reinforce their strengths as leaders.

- Mentorship extends far beyond an individual's role as an employee to challenges that reward the whole person. Success in a mentorship enriches an individual's life.

- Success in a mentorship depends on the willingness of both individuals to take risks, reveal their vulnerabilities, and trust each other to provide support in the relationship. The relationship demands loyalty to each other not as employees of a particular organization but as autonomous individuals.

- Ultimately, mentorships are relationships of trust. Mentors trust that the time, effort, insight, and wisdom that they impart will be well considered and applied constructively; mentees trust that they are forming and strengthening a nurturing relationship whose guidance and support will continue forever.

As the world emerges from a prolonged period of COVID-related disruption, fear, and apprehension, we face a future that will be vastly different than the past. To make our way fearlessly into this unknown future, we need more than ever to draw from the sustaining relationships between mentors and mentees.

The analyses and stories compiled in the following pages by Alan Middleton bring mentorships to life and show how they can contribute not just to better lives for mentors and mentees but also to a better world.

David Kincaid
Craig Lund
Co-chairs Mentor Exchange, American Marketing Association, Toronto Chapter (AMA Toronto)

PREFACE

"If I have seen further, it is by standing on the shoulders of giants"

– Isaac Newton, 1643–1727, British mathematician and scientist

The American Marketing Association Toronto chapter (AMA Toronto) has been a leader in Canadian management and in North American marketing in recognizing the importance of mentoring in the development of skilled, thoughtful, and effective managers. Since founding its Mentor Exchange in 2010, AMA Toronto has established a highly professional and successful process that has helped match and train over 500 mentors and mentees in marketing.

Mentoring is important in all aspects of marketing be it overall brand management, product and service development, channel strategy and management, pricing strategy and implementation, staff and customer service strategy, and management of all aspects of marketing communication. Marketing is a blend of art and science requiring a balance between learning and experience. Further, that balance varies by sector (private, public, and not-for-profit), industry type (e.g., financial services, information technology, retail, foodservice, manufacturing, healthcare, security and protection services, etc.) and time and location. That balance is best enabled by personal experience, formal learning, and most importantly, mentoring, counsel, and support from others with experience.

Recently, the effects of the COVID-19 pandemic have accelerated changes in management style. Organization hierarchies are flattening, technology has enabled work from home, and customers and citizens expect more personalized service. These changes place increased responsibility on front-line personnel to ensure their organization's success through initiative, goal setting, and teamwork across departmental silos. As such personnel need to be involved, motivated, trained, and developed better than ever before, which means mentoring is an even more critical management process for both mentors and mentees.

This short text is an update on where mentorship practices currently stand. It is not a detailed "how to." That is well covered in books like *10 Steps to Successful Mentoring* by Wendy Axelrod, *Mentoring: Mindset, Skills and Tools* by Ann Rolfe, and *Mentoring Programs That Work* by Jenn Labin. Rather, it is intended as a review and guide to the importance of mentorship programs in marketing for policy decision making during the post-pandemic era.

It is also a tribute to AMA Toronto—a wonderful example of the effectiveness and importance of volunteer organizations and to those involved with founding and directing the Mentor Exchange for over a decade. Thanks to all, but a special call out to David Pullara, who started on this written journey with me, and to Craig Lund who has contributed massively to AMA Toronto in general and to Mentor Exchange specifically. Others deserving of thanks for their invaluable contributions include:

- My Mentor Exchange Executive Committee colleagues over the last decade: Tony Chapman, Lynne Clarke, Stephen Graham, Rubina Havlin, David Kincaid, Craig Lund, Deb McKenzie, Matt McKenzie, Barbara Smith, Yasmin Pallan, David Pullara, Jim Warrington, and Maclin Williams

- The AMA Toronto President in 2020/21, Miglena Nikolova

- My fellow inductees into the AMA Marketing Hall of Legends in the Mentor category: Ken Wong, Rupert Brendon, Peter Zarry,

Allan Kazmer, Marlene Hore, Jim Barnes, Paula Gignac, Stefan Danis, Syd Kessler, Marshall McLuhan, and Richard Peddie

Become a mentor—but always seek to be a mentee to keep learning and growing.

Alan Middleton
June 2021

"Mentoring is a brain to pick, an ear to listen, and a push in the right direction"

– John Crosby, 1931–2020, Canadian Federal and Provincial politician

International Mentoring Day, January 17

Mentoring teaches us to lift each other up, creating powerful positive long-lasting relationships along the way. Mentoring reinforces the benefits of enhancing the lives of all people and can be especially uplifting for individuals who are isolated, excluded, or at the margins. Mentoring has and will continue to contribute toward fostering development, peace, and human rights. Mentoring can build a more inclusive and better world for all.

Mentoring is a powerful tool for raising awareness and understanding diversity and inclusion, helping us to recognize the importance of advocacy and being advocates for ourselves and others. Mentoring, whether formal or informal, reinforces the power of relationships and contributes to creating a better world.

Mentoring relationships help us to broaden our lens for diversity and inclusion, allowing us to see others as people first while moving beyond labels and stereotypes. Mentors and mentees can help each other to redefine "normal" and move to "typical," creating visibility for individuals or communities previously living as invisible to the greater society. Through mentorship, we can expand our minds, hearts, and vision toward race, sexual orientation, disability, religion, and culture. This is the power of mentoring. All are welcome in the mentoring space.

Contributed by Eli A. Wolff and Mary A. Hums in recognition of International Mentoring Day, January 17, 2021

INTRODUCTION

"The delicate art of mentoring someone is not creating them in your own image but giving them the opportunity to create themselves."

– Stephen Spielberg, 1946-date, American Oscar-winning film director, producer, screenwriter

With the changes wrought by the 2020/21 COVID-19 pandemic and the continuing improvement of communications and other technologies, the behaviours of everyone working in organizations is changing. One set of behaviours that will change is how mentorship practices are utilized. The mentorship process will become an ever more important management behaviour at all levels. This text reviews the literature and provides interview advice about how to work in this new environment.

It will address four questions you might have:

- What is mentoring about in the post-pandemic world?

- Why is being a mentor a key management skill at all levels?

- How can I be a mentee and learn how to improve my capabilities?

- How to mentor groups so that they can self-manage effectively without too much traditional-style bureaucratic regulation, rules and senior management direction?

This publication's objectives are to provide some answers, to give examples and insights, and to help you along whichever of the four journeys in which you are most interested.

Its objectives are twofold:

i To build on the extensive and excellent work on mentoring that has been published and experienced in organizations in the private, public, and not-for-profit sectors

ii To position the mentorship ability as an increasingly essential skill for executives and managers in the post-pandemic era

During 2020/21 the work world changed. The global Covid-19 pandemic caused healthcare issues amongst all, and especially the elderly. In 220 countries with 210 million infected, over 4.4 million dying, and the race to develop, source, approve, and distribute vaccines, it has impacted everyone. In Canada alone we have seen some 1.5 million infected and 27,000 deaths.

But it is not just our health that has been impacted. As many have commented, it has had major effects on the way we work. Combined with increasing applications of technology in all areas, but particularly communication, it has caused, or at least significantly accelerated, changes in the way we work together to achieve organizational and personal goals. For example, it is estimated that by 2025 70% of employees will be working remotely at least five days/month; a number reflected in Canadian and U.S. research that indicates only 17% of office-based staff expect to be onsite only. Scheduling remote with collocated work will become an important HR role. Performance management and motivation will change. An organization's reputation as a "good place to work" will become ever more important in attracting and retaining the best talent. All this will mean successful mentorship style relationships at work will become even more important.

Many impacts have already been seen:

- Service sectors – the majority of GDP activity in Canada and other OECD nations – employees in financial services, government, education, real estate, sports/art/cultural operations, learned to work from home via phone, email, social media, and especially video meetings ("zooming" has now become common parlance).

- Sectors like healthcare, emergency services, retail, transportation/logistics/supply chain, manufacturing, construction, and mining have continued at the workplace but with significant changes. These have been caused by technology, particularly AI, and the need for new balances of part-time and full-time employment.

- These have all changed employer/employee relations.

Before the pandemic there was much talk about the importance of the front-line employee, but organizations still tended to treat them as followers of management process and procedure determined by the organizational hierarchy. It's an old, Industrial-era 1.0 model.

Additionally, in most countries training in job roles is still mostly executional and not focused on developing and engaging them in goal setting, goal achievement, and working with others within and across organizational silos.

With the health, economic, and social impacts caused by covid-19 and the acceleration in the availability and use of improved technology, there is a need for a new, post–Industrial era thinking about organizations and their people. Gary Hamel and Michele Zanini have described the costs of bureaucracy and traditional organization behaviour, and have indicated a new way of working in their 2020 book Humanocracy.

Here are the contrasts:

Bureaucracy

- Power is vested in positions
- Strategy is set at the top

- Resources allocated by fiat
- Innovation as a specialized activity
- Mandates & policy force coordination
- People slotted into roles
- Managers assign tasks
- Control comes from oversight & rules
- Staff groups are monopoly service providers
- Individuals compete for promotion
- Units judged against top-down targets
- Compensation correlates with rank
- Employees have little financial upside
- There are ranks of managers
- Critical trade-offs are made at the top

Humanocracy
- Influence is earned from peers
- Strategy is an open firm-wide conversation
- Resources allocated by market mechanism
- Innovation—everyone's job
- Coordination from collaboration
- Roles built round individual skills
- Teams divide up work
- Control comes from transparency and peers
- Staff groups compete against external vendors
- Individuals compete to add value

- Units are responsible for local P&Ls
- Compensation correlates with impact
- Employees have significant financial upside
- Self-managing teams/individuals
- Critical trade-offs optimized locally

What is clear in this shift is that the old concepts of hierarchy and management rules must change. The ability to mentor and nudge become much more effective then direct and order.

It is in this context of an accelerated rate of change caused by learning during the pandemic and improvements in technology that we must view the role of mentorship as a key management skill at all levels. In the first case, this is exactly how Bob Froese's management style evolved.

Introductory Case: A Mentor's Perspective

Interview with Bob Froese, Co-founder and CEO of Bob's Your Uncle for 25 years, a successful advertising agency with accounts like Popeyes Louisiana Kitchen. Mentor with AMA Toronto Mentor Exchange and recognized as "Mentor of the Year" in 2016.

Brought up in Winnipeg, and after an early experience with IT consulting, Bob got into advertising with McKim, then Publicis before co-founding his own advertising agency in Toronto in 1995. Expanding internationally during the early 2000s, for the last 10 years they have remained a most successful Toronto agency focusing on food and beverage brands.

Bob's mentorship journey started early as a mentee but with a client in his agency:

"My first mentoring experience occurred many years ago with one of my clients who was head of marketing for Mr. Lube at the time. This was a significant national account for our agency and I was just young in advertising. I was awestruck by how much faith he was prepared to put in my advice. But I also realized that he was guiding me quite carefully while he was asking for my opinions. It was a five-year relationship and I just learned so much."

This experience helped establish an ideal for Bob, so when he founded his own advertising agency, he took with him a number of the lessons learned when dealing with his own staff. As he indicates, while many of these were not formal mentorship relationships, he just looked for these types of relationships as they emerged.

The value in the mentorship relationship to Bob is this:

"You can build a lot of confidence [for the mentees] so that people can do much more than they think. Most people don't give themselves enough credit for what they can do. It is about finding ways to hear what your mentee is saying and reflect it back to them with some guidance that will give them 'heart', confidence, and purpose. And as a mentor I was surprised about how much value came back to me. It really, really felt reciprocal. I felt I got every bit out whatever I put into it."

The process to Bob is, then, reflections and a reminder of how much one has learned and experienced and how energizing it can be to pass it on. And it continues—many of the great relationships Bob has had continue for years afterward.

Bob also found the disciplines he learned in the Mentor Exchange program most helpful in structuring his relationships but at the heart of a great relationship was still *"being genuine about your interest in the person."*

In his most successful relationships he found, and encouraged, mentees who would decide on some actions to take, and then by the next meeting had worked on them and in many cases succeeded with them. It was *"a mutual commitment to achieve the goals."*

Bob has been less worried about mentee matching based on gender, race or religion but thinks the values and goals in the match have determined his most successful experiences.

He also reflected on how the management style of his company over 25 years had evolved from more formal systems with reporting points, performance reviews, status meetings that described process, time sheets and so on, to a more informal, goal setting and achievement orientation.

Their weekly meetings are now as follows:

"Monday, three things they [the staff] want to accomplish and on Friday what has been accomplished. Additionally, they are required to give a shout out to another employee who has accomplished or lived the cultural values of the organization."

Bob sees the keys to successful mentorship experiences as the following:

- *"You have to take it seriously: the issues are a really big deal for the mentee."*

- A genuine desire to help somebody: satisfaction about giving back.

- Some formality in meeting times and goal setting.

- There is a mix of coaching and mentoring, but coaching is more directive, while mentoring is more about listening and guiding.

- Measures of success should be specific to each relationship, but these do need to be discussed. A good measure is the level of personal confidence and fulfilment by the mentee and *"what they believe they can now accomplish."*

Bob has also had experience with peer group meetings, including an association of North American agency heads and entrepreneurship organizations (like the CEO Global Network). While these have some elements of mentoring, he believes they work in a different way: more sharing and listening to other experiences rather than individually focused conversation.

As Bob describes the key to the mentor–mentee relationship, it is:

"Commitment to each other. With that you can work on everything else."

Interview: February 23, 2021

1

MENTORING: WHAT IT IS, WHAT IT ISN'T, AND WHAT IT IS BECOMING

"In what is known as the 70/20/10 learning concept, 70% of learning and development takes place from real-time and on-the-job experiences, tasks and problem-solving, 20% comes from other people through informal or formal feedback, mentoring or coaching, and 10% from formal training."

– Robert Eichinger, Michael Lombardi, Morgan McCall, Centre for Creative Leadership

This chapter has a brief review of what has been written about the origins and evolving nature of mentoring.

Harvard Business Review Press in their *Coaching and Mentoring* book defines mentoring as follows: "Mentoring is the offering of advice, information, or guidance by a person with useful experience, skills or expertise for another individual's personal and professional development."

The word *mentor* comes from a character in Greek mythology portrayed in Homer's *Odyssey*. Mentor was actually Athena, the goddess of wisdom in disguise, entrusted to educate Telemachus, the son of Odysseus. Mentor's job was to guide the development of Prince Telemachus while Odysseus was fighting in the Trojan Wars. Telemachus needed to be prepared to be the future ruler of the kingdom. As Homer expressed the relationship:

> *"For you, I have some good advice, if only you will accept it."*
> *"Oh stranger", heedful Telemachus replied, "Indeed I will. You have counselled me with so much kindness now, like a father a son. I will not forget a word."*

The first use of *mentor* in the modern (or near-modern) era appeared in the 18th century in the work of the French author Francis Fenelon in his *Adventures of Telemachus* followed by the English version of de Caraccioli's *The True Mentor, or An Essay on the Education of Young People of Fashion* in 1760.

Across global cultures and religions there have been similar types of relationships: the roles of a guru or spiritual leader, councils of elders in many indigenous groups, or guilds. Indeed, guilds dating back to fourteenth century Europe had a recognized progression based on experience, learning and mentorship from apprenticeship to craftsman to journeyman to master.

Throughout history there have been many famous mentor–mentee relationships:

Socrates and Plato

Plato and Aristotle

Joseph Haydn and Ludwig van Beethoven

Henri Becquerel and Marie Curie

Sigmund Freud and Carl Jung

Mahatma Gandhi and Nelson Mandela

Benjamin Mays and Martin Luther King

Benjamin Graham and Warren Buffett

Warren Buffett and Bill Gates

Andy Grove and Steve Jobs

Steve Jobs and Marc Benioff (salesforce.com)

Maya Angelou and Oprah Winfrey

Larry Summers and Sheryl Sandberg

There are many other historical figures who stand out for their leadership and the ability to influence and impact others. An incomplete list would include great historical leaders like Catherine II (the Great) of Russia, Winston Churchill, Marie Curie, Elizabeth I of England, Albert Einstein, Hatshepsut of Egypt, Nelson Mandela, Golda Meir, Florence Nightingale, Emmeline Pankhurst, Rosa Parks, Franklin D. Roosevelt, Tecumseh, and Deng Xiaoping. An expanded list could also include more contemporary leaders like Jacinda Arden, Stephen Hawking, Angela Merkel, Mother Teresa, Margaret Thatcher, and Lee Kuan Yew.

There's more: contemporary business leaders like Mary Barra, Tim Cook, Marvin Ellison, Reed Hastings, Bob Iger, Jack Ma, Huateng 'Pony' Ma, Ginni Rometty, Ratan Tata, and Susan Wojcicki are also staking their claim. In addition, in the arts and entertainment industry Viola Davis has been a mentor to Meryl Streep and Nora Ephron a mentor to Lena Dunham, and there are reports of many others.

The modern use of mentorship came from work on the education of young people by Gail Sheely in 1976 and David Levinson in 1979. This is why early adaptations beyond education focused on early career managers and employees. As will be seen in later chapters, this approach has evolved.

Mentoring is generally regarded as having both career and psychosocial functions. Career functions include:

- Sponsorship: opening doors that might otherwise be closed

- Coaching: teaching and feedback

- Protection: supporting and acting as a buffer of criticism

- Challenge: encouraging new ways of thinking and acting; pushing the mentee to stretch their capabilities

- Exposure and visibility: increasing awareness of mentee capabilities

    Psychosocial functions include:

- Role modeling: demonstrating kinds of successful behaviours, attitudes and values

- Counselling: help with difficult dilemmas

- Acceptance and confirmation: supporting and giving respect

- Friendship: personal caring

Mentoring Within an Organization (Internal) or Outside (External)

Mentoring is mostly associated with internal organization relations, especially with a recently emphasized focus on sponsorship (with which the author has concerns). However, external mentorships are developing rapidly especially in areas of:

- Professional or specialist knowledge groups like law, education, HR, marketing, real estate, etc. (e.g., AMA Toronto's Mentor Exchange, ULI Toronto Mentorship Program)
- Specific demographic groups like women's mentorship programs (e.g., Women's Executive Network)
- Specific industry sector groups like not-for-profit, entrepreneurship (e.g., Micromentor)

These relationships have the advantage of being less political than internal mentoring and are more psychosocial in emphasis. They suffer the obvious disadvantage of being less directly utilitarian in internal career management.

The author believes that there is room, indeed a need, for both types.

Internal mentoring done well aids people through the competencies, knowledge, judgement needed within a specific organization. By being specific to the organization, it can focus on the disciplines and managerial skills judged to be essential to the organization's success. Great examples can be seen in this book in Cases 1.1, 4.1, and 4.3.

The newer emphasis on sponsorship where the mentor is more actively and directly involved in the career progression of the mentee sounds attractive. However, this author is concerned that it shifts the focus of the relationship too much towards the mentor as it tempts them to hold on to high potentials as both staff for themselves as well as their mentees. Legitimate internal mentoring keeps the balance between delivering value to the mentee with a minimal level of internal politics while still being valuable to the mentor and the organization.

External mentoring allows a greater focus on the discipline and general industry perspective, but clearly is less able to handle the internal knowledge, culture, and politics of the mentee's organization.

Formal and Informal Mentoring

Mentoring can and does happen naturally. The mentoring process can therefore be part of a formal process either internally or externally or informal. The formal process internally often seeks to achieve specific goals. The informal process depends on who initiated the relationship. A similar contrast works externally though the goals may be a little less specific. The contrast is often as follows:

Informal Mentoring:

- Goals of the relationship often not specified

- Outcomes not measured

- Access limited and may be exclusive

- Mentors and mentees self-select on the basis of personal chemistry and/or reputation

- Mentoring often becomes very long term, sometimes a lifetime

- The organization benefits indirectly

Formal Mentoring:

- Goals established from the beginning by the employee mentee with input from the mentor and the organization's program

- Outcomes are measured

- Access open to all who meet program criteria

- Mentors and mentees paired based on matching and compatibility

- Training and support in mentoring is provided

One of the more recent innovations (2013) in external informal mentoring has been the software organization "Ten Thousand Coffees," a program aimed at young people where some 300-plus senior leaders, including such individuals as Chris Hadfield, Justin Trudeau, John

Ruffolo, Tim Hockey, Karen Stintz, and Rick Mercer, offer an advisory meeting over coffee to young people.

Mentorship Audiences

Part of the growth in mentoring activities in the last couple of decades has been to encourage acceleration of talent development amongst more diverse audiences. Organizations previously had senior cultures of primarily white boomer males. With the need to develop a broader audience in age, gender and ethnic background, formal internal and external mentorship programs have developed specifically to aid these groups.

Organizations that achieve real diversity in their programs are those that better address the needs for innovation and effective knowledge transfer with *all* staff.

Coaching vs. Mentoring

There is often confusion between mentoring and coaching. HBR Press's *Coaching and Mentoring*, with additions from this author, clarifies the difference:

	Coaching	Mentoring
Key Goals	Correct inappropriate behavior, improve performance, impart appropriate skills.	Support and guide personal growth.
Initiative	Coach directs learning and instruction.	Mentee-driven agenda.
Volunteerism	Subordinate generally agrees to accept instruction.	Both Mentor and Mentee are volunteers.
Focus	Immediate problems and learning opportunities.	Longer-term career and personal development.
Roles	Telling with some feedback.	Listening, with some suggestions and corrections.
Duration	As needed but concentrated.	Continuous and longer term.
Relationship	Coach is boss or recognized superior in skill.	Rarely the direct boss.
Organization	Generally structured and regular meetings.	More informal and both regular and when mentee needs advice.

The Role of Mentorship

Why is mentorship such an important management process? Studies in the psychology of learning indicate that the flow of learning is as follows:

1. Concrete experience   2. Reflection   3. Abstract Conception
4. Action

Coaching and mentoring assist in the transition from experience through this learning process to newer/better thinking and action. It helps transformational consciousness and behaviour. Essentially the mentor offers the mentee:

- A sounding board
- Facilitation of access to networks of people and information
- Advisor in career and personal development matters

In terms of talent development, think of a four-legged table with the legs supporting effective leadership:

- Experience

- Formal learning

- Informal learning

- Mentoring/coaching

We need all four legs for a stable table to be able to access the resources and information for work and personal life. In our work life, this helps not only to perform current roles better but to also prepare for new roles and responsibilities. In personal life, this leads to a healthy balance of time and contribution to work, family and social life, and personal time.

Recent management training data in North America indicates that we are becoming more short term in our learning demands; we are looking for quicker returns, more instant gratification. This trend toward shorter-term training that enables skill development for current roles does not address future career development or important work-life balance issues. From an employer viewpoint this is already causing problems and is a reason why succession planning and talent development are becoming two priorities in HR and talent management departments.

Employers need to pay attention to mentorship programs, as they not only aid in performance in current roles but also in development for future roles. An Addison Group research report quoted by Stephanie Vozza indicated that in a 2014 survey of over 1,000 boomers, Gen-X, and millennials that 63% of managers do prefer to lead through mentorship. The same survey indicated that millennials preferred more personal relationships: 20% strove to become their boss's best friend. This is important, as research indicates that millennials are motivated to work because they like their boss.

For the individual, either as a mentor or mentee, both performance in a current role and developmental needs are best served by feasting off a stable four-legged table.

When is Mentorship Needed Most?

While there tends to be a higher need for mentorship and coaching early in one's career, the (Peter) Hawkins model suggests a continuing need throughout a person's career.

The model suggest four career stages:

Career stage	Core concern	Common age span
Experimentation	Who am I in the world of work?	16 – 35 years old.
Experience accumulation	Gaining credibility/track record, growing the cv..	20 – 40 years old.
Full leadership	Making a difference and leaving a legacy..	30 – 60 years old.
Eldership	Enabling others, passing the torch, stewardship.	50 – 90 years old.

There are five identifiable phases in each stage of the mentoring process:

1. Rapport
2. Direction
3. Progression
4. Maturation
5. Closure

As evidenced in the interviews in this book, sometimes these relationships take place over many years, and there are different ways to maximize the value of the relationship at the different phases.

Attributes of Great Mentors

- They get pleasure from developing others.
- They are proud of, not threatened by, the accomplishments of others.
- They are good at "reading" people and situations.
- They know the organization/industry/professional discipline from experience, training, and mentoring and can balance these capabilities with the needs of the individual mentee.
- They are tolerant and encouraging of individual differences: personality, values, age, gender, and ethnic backgrounds.
- They look forward to giving something back and making a difference.
- They reward efforts and actions (do not praise intelligence, rather praise perseverance, effort, improvement and accomplishment).
- They have a generous, optimistic spirit.
- Typically, they are not the mentee's boss.

Successful mentors help build more loyal teams: a Lou Harris study indicated 35% of new employees without the benefit of mentoring started looking for a new job versus 16% of those who had capable mentors.

Attributes of Great Mentees

- High potential
- Interested in developing skills, competencies, and knowledge
- Open to help/advice
- Capable of progressing
- Able and willing to partner in their growth

Benefits of Mentoring to the Organization

Three major benefits emerge from the literature:

i   Developing human assets: along with previous experience, mentorship along with current experience and training and development adds capability to the people in the organization.

ii   Transfer of tacit knowledge: mentoring enables transfer of tacit knowledge (knowledge that is difficult to codify or store—often the results of judgement) from the experienced to the less experienced.

iii   Retention of the "right" people: by increasing the knowledge and capabilities of both mentors and mentees, mentoring can help the quality of the work environment and thereby aid retention of good people at all levels.

Mentorship works for all involved, not just the mentee but for the mentor and the organization.

Mentorship: Evidence of Effectiveness

The case for the importance of mentorship along with experience and training lies with the imperative for organizations to achieve successful innovation, improved productivity, greater efficiency and improved cost management in order to remain competitive. In an organization a manager's skill and motivation are essential ingredients of success in achieving organizational goals. Mentoring arrangements can provide an essential motivational ingredient. Additionally, the need to engage and motivate at all levels, all genders, and all ethnic backgrounds and not waste talent is an increasing imperative and the reason behind the growth in external mentoring groups.

Typically support for effectiveness lies in case histories. A book like Ho Law's *The Psychology of Coaching, Mentoring and Learning* contains cases from many sources. These indicate the main benefits for both mentors and mentees lie in the areas of motivational aptitude, knowledge, skills development, managing change and succession, and business performance benefits.

Specifically mentioned are:

- Motivational benefits: career advancement, improved commitment to business and organization improvement, improved job satisfaction, and increased income.

- Knowledge and skills development for mentees: improved abilities and skills, faster learning, enhanced decision making, and improved understanding of business and organizational workings (policies, politics, greater ability for risk taking, and innovation).

- Managing change and succession: gains in confidence and well-being in leadership roles for mentees and for mentors enhanced the understanding of others' perspectives, improved communication, self-awareness, job satisfaction and loyalty, and rejuvenation.

- Organization benefits include reduction in staff turnover, improvement in retention, improved flow of communication, better opportunity for talent development, improvement in organizational learning, increased knowledge transfer, effective and cost-effective addition to training.

Newer Directions

Mentorship has evolved in recent years. Driven by changes in global business patterns, greater and better diversity in leadership roles and new and evolving technologies, these have been accelerated recently by such issues as:

- Flattening organizational hierarchies to reduce bureaucracy and speed, and improve decision-making and market responsiveness.

- Gradual recognition that those with direct customer contact or production contact are more aware of problems, improvement opportunities and needed changes, and should be encouraged and rewarded to input and execute improvement ideas.

- Diversity of workforce that, managed well, can improve creativity and innovation.

- Diversity of working habits: blending in-office/workplace and on-line from home.

- Greater mixtures of full-time and contract staff.

- Greater pressure from staff for employers to recognize the need for work life/home life balance.

- Increasing recognition of the importance for staff productivity of staff satisfaction that aids in hiring better talent. This is now reinforced by published surveys such as:

  - Canada's Top 100 Employers 2021 by *The Globe and Mail* include organizations such as 3M, BDC, CIBC, Loblaws, L'Oreal, Shopify, and Toyota.

  - Canada's Best Employers 2021 by Forbes include organizations such as Cisco, CIBC, FedEx, IBM, Scotiabank, Shopify, and Ubisoft.

- o Canada's Top Employers for Young People 2020 include organizations such as CGI, CIBC, Hatch, Hospital for Sick Children, Manulife, Rogers, Scotiabank, and Telus.

- o *Fortune* 100 Best Companies to Work For 2020 include organizations such as Hilton, Wegmans, Cisco, Salesforce, and Amex.

- o *Fortune* Best Workplaces in Retail 2020: Wegmans and Target.

Newer research, cases, and literature indicate the value of recent developments to meet the changing environment:

- Mentorship—both giving and receiving—is now viewed as a key management skill.

- Mentorship from people with similar gender/ethnic backgrounds has been on the increase given the previous experience-oriented models that tended to have a white, male predominance. These are indeed of major value but increasingly the value of the mentor will be more determined by experience, perspective, and motivation regardless of gender/ethnic background.

- It is now much more a two-way experience between mentor and mentee: each has value to each other albeit in different ways.

- Mentorship can be to a group and within a group as well as individual to individual. In fact, given the world described earlier in *Humanocracy*, this group/team orientation may be one of the most important new developments.

In her book *"Mentoring"* Ann Rolfe makes the following contrast:

Traditional Paradigm	Contemporary Thinking
Mentor picks a protegee.	Mentee looks for mentors.
Mentor is more senior.	Mentor is someone you can learn from regardless of age/position.
Mentor should have much in common with mentee.	Differences provide greater opportunity for discovery, challenge and growth.
Mentoring is for young people.	Mentoring can be helpful at any stage.
You have one mentor.	You have mentors for different aspects and life and career.
Mentoring is one-to-one.	Mentoring may be individual or a group.
Mentor tells you what to do.	Mentor is a sounding board.
Mentors give advice.	Mentors assist your decision-making and problem-solving.
You are either a Mentor or Mentee	You can be either or both.

Ann Rolfe's definition is much more in keeping with the contemporary organizational world:

"A mentor enables the mentee to move towards their chosen goals with the benefit of their own insight and (possibly) advice or input based on the mentor's experience."

Conclusion

This chapter has sought to set the background to mentoring: a little about its history, its scope, its workings, and its importance in the contemporary organization. As recent articles have pointed out, leadership is about developing and helping individuals and teams without micromanaging. Good mentorship practices emphasize the timing of the involvement to meet the mentee's needs, indicating that the involvements are suggestions not instructions and that mentees (individual or team) own the initiative as to how to engage.

The two cases that follow illustrate two approaches: a widely diverse internal approach and a highly successful external program.

Case #1.1. In-company Mentorship Programs: CIBC

CIBC is a leading North American financial institution with 10 million personal banking, business, public sector, and institutional clients. It offers a full range of advice, solutions, and services in Personal and Business Banking, Commercial Banking and Wealth Management, and Capital Markets businesses. These are available through its leading digital banking network and locations across Canada and offices in the United States and around the world.

Interview with John R. Silverthorn, Senior Vice President CIBC HR Advisory Services and Talent Development.

John Silverthorn has an extensive, successful career in Human Resources and Talent Development. For the past 15 years he has been a leader in the development of CIBC leaders including senior executives, managers at all levels and high-potential employees. Currently he leads the HR Generalist and Employee/Labour Relations Specialists team that supports all CIBC strategic businesses and functional groups. Prior to joining CIBC, John had a successful 20-year career with IBM leading HR operations in Canada, the United States, and Latin America. IBM is well known for its extensive mentorship programs and in 2008 had a book published on its methods titled *Intelligent Mentoring: How IBM Creates Value through People, Knowledge, and Relationships.*

John shared that:

"CIBC's talent development has traditionally focused on the 3 E's: Education, Experience, and Exposure. Exposure encompasses learning from others through formal apprenticeships, "buddy systems" for new senior executives, and mentorships. Recently we have added a fourth "E" focused on Environment, which reinforces the importance of learning and responding in the moment."

CIBC has no formal, organization-wide mentorship program, as its philosophy is built into all of its talent development strategies. This approach fits the needs of the different business lines at CIBC. John gives five examples of their approach to internal and external mentorship programs:

First are business unit specific programs. As an example, CIBC's Credit Adjustment Group helps their representatives with their underwriting skills where they are assigned formal mentors.

Second, high-potential senior middle managers are assigned senior executive mentors.

Third, for very senior new executives a "buddy system" pairs them with someone who can help them orient themselves to CIBC's culture and the people of the organization throughout their first year on board.

"This establishes a safe, confidential environment which enables the newcomer to ask, observe, and speak about the culture."

Fourth, and perhaps the example of which John is most proud, is CIBC's relationship with the Toronto Region Immigrant Employment Council (TRIEC) where CIBC leaders mentor recent immigrants to learn about the national culture and how to effectively navigate job searches. This external exposure is hugely valuable for both the mentee and the mentor, as John comments:

"Recent immigrant qualifications are very often extremely strong. However, they need help to understand the best way to find jobs that use those qualifications and their true talents. Equally, the value to our mentors is considerable as they learn more about this aspect of our community, which helps them to be better leaders in our workplace."

Fifth, and with another link to an external organization, is CIBC's sponsorship of the Women's Executive Network (WXN). CIBC female executives work with WXN and get 10 formal mentorship spots and 10 peer-to-peer opportunities.

In addition to the five examples John cites there is the CIBC Youthvision Scholarship. As part of this 30 Grade 10 "at risk" students receive scholarships and mentorships with Big Brother, Big Sister, and the YMCA.

Additionally, CIBC employees are provided guides on how to get the most out of affinity groups and mentorship circles. Known as CIBC People Networks, these include CIBC Asian Employee Network and Indigenous Employee Circle, which includes activities with organizations like Indspire, Teach for Canada, Martin Family Initiative and the Canadian Council for Aboriginal Business. Others include

CIBC Black Employee Network, International Professionals Network, Latin Network, NextGen Network (for young professionals), Pride Network (for LGBTQ), WorkAbility Network, CIBC South Asian Employee Network, and Women's Network.

Linked to the mentorship philosophy are a couple of programs for new or junior employees:

- A speed dating mentorship event where, once a year, junior employees donate to the United Way to spend time with a senior employee.

- The Graduates Matter Rotation Program (GMRP), with four six-month rotation programs for newly hired graduates where each will be assigned a mentor for the program.

John is a fan of these extended but less centralized and formal programs. In his view, over-centralized initiatives can become too bureaucratic and can sometimes add confusion, as employees looking for mentors become too focused on sponsorship.

"When we see employees focusing myopically on the level and status of their mentor, we know individuals are seeking help for their career advancement more than mentorship."

John sees tremendous value in both internal programs and in external programs as well. Ideally mentorship should be a mix of *"give-back and development for the mentors as well as learning from others for the mentees."*

Interview: March 12, 2021

Case #1.2. External Mentorship Program – AMA Toronto

AMA Toronto Mentor Exchange is a case of a leading external mentorship program: turning the business talent of today into the leaders of tomorrow. Running since 2010 and with over 550 alumni mentees and 250 alumni mentors, the AMA Toronto Mentor Exchange is one of the most successful external mentorship programs in North America. Targeted at people in the broad field of marketing, it has become an essential management developmental opportunity for both mentees and mentors in the marketing industry.

Interview with David Kincaid, Co-Chair of Mentor Exchange, Founder & Managing Partner, Level5 Strategy Group and Craig Lund, Co-Chair of Mentor Exchange, Secretary and VP Mentorship AMA Toronto, and Founder and President, Marketing Talent Inc.

In 2004, AMA Toronto founded Canada's Marketing Hall of Legends (CMHOL) to recognize great leaders in marketing and continue to promote marketing as an essential business discipline in Canada. It proved extremely successful. However, AMA Toronto recognized that to fully develop effective marketers, leaders should not only be recognized for their backgrounds, experience and viewpoints, but *all levels* needed to be continually developed. As Craig and others have noted, management in general, and especially marketing, is an art/science mixture. While there were formal education programs at Universities and Colleges, there were few available developmental opportunities outside of a formal coaching consultancy that enabled people of experience to pass along the value of their experience. The idea was simple: to have those recognized leaders transfer the value of their experience to others with less experience.

In 2010, past AMA Toronto President's Deborah McKenzie and Jim Warrington were asked to launch this new mentorship initiative and dubbed it the "Mentor Exchange" to act as an extension of CMHOL. Thus began the development of a pilot program with a small amount of funding from AMA Toronto and a small fee paid by each of the initial 50 mentees.

As Craig indicates, "At the time there were some internal mentorship programs but when we looked around there were no external ones specifically for marketing professionals."

Key decisions made then were:

- After the first year, David Kincaid and Craig Lund were appointed to manage and develop the program to be more robust and self-sustaining. An Advisory Council was formed with some inductees from Canada's Marketing Hall of Legends, other prominent marketing leaders, and mentor and mentee representatives who had benefited from the first year of the Mentor Exchange program. This group started program refinements.

- To be sure, the program was still affordable for mentees—but also affordable for a volunteer organization like AMA Toronto to run—the fee was increased from $50 to $250, which allowed for more scheduled programming to be included such as a launch reception, networking events, and a formal graduation.

- Annual customer experience research was initiated and conducted through research partner Hotspex. This allowed the Advisory Council to gain insight into the satisfaction of the mentor–mentee matching quality and to understand why some matches were so highly rated and others less so.

- Based on this input, the decision was made to classify mentors and mentees to achieve more satisfactory matches. The agreed classifications were: Client Savant, Agency Savant, Client/Agency crossover, Educator, Entrepreneur, and Consultant. This covered the general spectrum of careers within the industry.

- It was agreed to set a substantial experience criterion for both mentors but also mentees. Mentors had to be recognized leaders in their organizations and the community. Mentees had to be at least 30 years old and have 8+ years of work experience. The program did not target the newly employed, as its goal was to provide important value for mentees at a later key career stage and provide value for mentors so that they would continue their involvement. This last point was a key finding from the research. Mentors with poor matches based on the mentee's lack of experience or engagement in the program were less likely to return to mentor the following year.

- A data scientist was appointed to continually upgrade the "matching engine" based on the ongoing research. The revised matching program allowed mentees to match against mentors with the desired background and experience and the advice or outcomes that they sought. Once the choice was made and the computer matching was conducted, a panel of experts reviewed the result for any final adjustments.

- Each year approximately 50 mentees were matched with mentors.

- At the five-year mark of Mentor Exchange it was recognized that to keep it evolving, four things had to happen: (1) greater value in terms of training and networking had to be offered; (2) economically, broader sponsorship was needed to offset costs; (3) the matching engine, while expensive, was essential to the program; and (4) the mentee fee needed to be more substantial: a daunting decision, but one which on the advice of the Advisory Council, enabled the program to further evolve.

- Along with the expanded benefits, the mentee fee was raised to $800 (though reduced during the pandemic period of 2020/21 by removing physical event costs), which entitled the mentee to:

  o A one-year global membership in the AMA.

  o Minimum of nine mentor meetings.

  o Professionally facilitated training programs for both mentee and mentor separately so that "safe space" learning and discussions could be held outside of the possible political environment of an internal program. This was provided through a highly regarded executive education provider, the Schulich Executive Education Centre.

  o Admission to AMA special events and networking opportunities in addition to the special launch and graduation receptions.

- The computer-matching program was continually improved.

- Sponsorship funding for the program was acquired. "Mentor Exchange" has had great sponsors from organizations like Hotspex and Loyalty One, as well as some like Scotiabank who had their own internal programs and saw this as a good "add-on" given its close alignment to their brand values.

As the reputation of the program spread, mentee applicants outnumbered the 50 spaces. With that choice of who to select, mentee quality improved and the mentor–mentee experience also improved reinforcing the positive experience for the mentors. Currently, about 70% of the mentors have previously been involved in the program either as mentors or mentees who have been successful in their careers. This mentor–mentee reverse mentoring has had huge advantages for all involved, not least of which has been the exploration of new technologies in marketing. This has been a vivid illustration of why mentorship relations have huge value to both mentee and mentor: the exchange of knowledge, experience, new learning, and leadership competencies.

In the case of the mentor, the value of these open discussions outside of one's own organization is well expressed by Craig:

"[Internally in an organizational relationship the situation may be that] *my people are not necessarily going to tell me bad things or complain about their job. Here they can say 'I spoke to somebody who is doing a similar job and they said here's how they struggle with these things.' And then they were able to have really valuable conversations within their own organization that came from the learning they had with their external mentee."*

The pandemic of 2020/21 meant that everything went online including mentor–mentee meetings. Communication of what to do and how to conduct meetings online increased and "check-in" communication was more frequent. With all program events moved to a virtual format, the mentee fee was reduced but the program continued to be strong.

In February 2018, AMA Toronto launched its "Career Accelerator" program designed to enable networking and learning for those earlier in their careers. Targeted at 24–30 year-olds in marketing with at least one-year work experience, for the yearly fee of under $200, it offers:

- A one-year global membership in AMA

- Five one-on-one mentorship meetings with a dedicated mentor

- A networking reception
- Access to AMA member-only networking opportunities

Regarding the more junior version of Mentor Exchange, it is a lite version of the main program, but it does recognize the need for networking and empowering aspiring leaders at an early career stage. It also provides mentee graduates from the Mentor Exchange program with the opportunity to develop and practice their own leadership and mentoring skills by becoming mentors in Career Accelerator.

Both Mentor Exchange and Career Accelerator are leveraged by a number of organizations with their own internal mentorship programs. That really emphasizes the value of an external program: organizations like Amex, Hasbro, PwC, and Scotiabank use it both as a developmental opportunity and as a reward for their top talent, and sponsor their employees' participation.

AMA Toronto's Mentor Exchange is a highly successful external program that shows the importance of mentorship practices. As Craig so well expresses it:

"The program is designed to elevate the individual in their career, to help them make decisions, grow within the role they have, and help them decide whether it is the right role for them. I have noticed that people managers, typically, are not prepared to be vulnerable with their teams.

What we now know is that for a mentorship to truly blossom and be fulfilling for everybody, there needs to be vulnerability... and especially around the other half of our life: our living and personal life. Managers are too often just focused on the work life; a mentor has a much farther horizon, so they are prepared to be vulnerable, and a lot of value is gained from doing that."

One of the references in this book, *Humanocracy*, discusses exactly why this view is an important one for the future. Well said, and thank you David and Craig.

Interview: February 10, 2021

2

BEING A GREAT MENTOR

"Mentoring is a two-way street. The mentor gets wiser while mentoring and the mentee gains knowledge."

— **Marisol Gonzalez, 1983–date, Mexican actor and TV personality**

Mentoring has typically been offered both formally and informally inside organizations. Historically this has tended to skew the mentor population by gender and ethnic background. Although this has changed in recent times, the demand for a broader representation led to the rise of external mentorship groups that addressed the needs for more diversity in mentorship. The evidence suggests each, internal and external, have advantages and disadvantages. We will examine both.

In addition, as individuals progress through their careers they are likely to be both mentor and mentee depending on their goals and needs. Accordingly, mentorship capability has become a key management skill at every management level and it is an important capability informally and formally. As one author (Rolfe) indicates, leadership and mentorship have merged. In the post-pandemic world this is more important than ever. As such, the "tips" and cases in this chapter apply to all.

I. The Internal Mentor

In the last couple of decades there has been a discernible increase in the number of internal mentorship programs. The reasons were briefly described in the previous chapter. Originally widely used in healthcare organizations, internal mentoring practices have been adopted extensively in private sector, not-for-profit, government, and educational institutions. The reason is the value that mentoring brings to both mentor and mentee, as well as to the organization itself: all have good reasons to get involved in internal mentorship relationships.

Mentors:

1. Improve their management skills: listening and asking, facilitating change management, influencing, and overcoming obstacles

2. Prove themselves as valuable leaders by learning what it takes to develop others

3. Gain fresh perspectives and stay updated and relevant with new thinking and knowledge

4. Learn more about themselves

5. Share expertise with others in the organization

6. Expand their professional network

7. Invest in the future of the organization.

8. Reinforce their role as subject matter experts.

Mentees:

1. Improve a particular career track

2. Learn about other divisions or opportunities in the organization

3. Explore potential for growth/career in untapped areas

4. For new hires, familiarize themselves with the organization

5. Make valuable contacts in the organization

6. Enhance career advancement opportunities

Organizations:

1. Helps create a culture that encourages personal and professional growth through the sharing of information, competencies, values, and behaviours

2. Role models: leaders building leaders

3. Helps the process of identification, development and retention of talent for key managerial and technical roles

4. Improves job satisfaction for both mentees and mentors

5. Enables sharing and leveraging of knowledge and experience

Advantages of Internal Mentoring programs

As the previous section indicated, many of the advantages of internal mentoring programs lie in the organization's commitment to providing a well-run program. Clearly, if this commitment exists and a full program is in place, then there are many strong advantages:

1. Highly relevant mentoring content that applies directly to the knowledge, competencies, skills, and perspectives necessary to succeed in the organization.

2. Valuable contact with senior executives acting as mentors.

3. Mentors and mentees gain huge communication and knowledge-transfer benefits.

4. Organizations with strong mentorship programs are likely to have cultures that respect talent training and development, thereby delivering the complete "four legs of the table" for career advancement.

5. Because of this positive culture of talent development, mentees gain from greater opportunities for internal promotion, mentors gain knowledge, perspective, and energy from younger talented mentees, and the organization gains from lower turnover and loss of valuable talent.

6. And there are multiple models of mentoring that organizations can adopt.

"Mentors at Caterpillar provide guidance on almost every aspect of in-house practice such as career exploration, corporate culture, 'soft skills' development, organizational understanding, internal enterprise awareness, work-life balance, and community knowledge."

– Jamie Meyers, Corporate Counsel, Caterpillar, Vince Scalia /Gloo podcast July 2019

Disadvantages of Internal Mentoring Programs

While organizations should have a mentorship program of some kind, not every organization has one. Additionally, not all organizations have one that is extensive and professionally managed. Those with less extensive and less well-managed programs may even be worse than no mentorship program due to:

1. Poor integration into talent development programs.

2. Experience bias of the mentors whose backgrounds may only be in the organization. This may limit knowledge, experience and perspective of the industry or professional discipline.

3. Inadequate mentor and/or mentee training or preparation.

4. Mentors/mentees may be too junior for the role.

5. Bad mentor–mentee "matching" processes.

6. Poor evaluation and/or follow up.

However, the most serious potential disadvantage of internal programs lies in politicization of the process:

1. Political bias due to background/cultural dominance (professional discipline, gender, age, ethnic background), which may distort the fairness and openness of the system and the relationships.

2. Political bias to the specific needs of the organization may distort the mentor's views and/or advice rather than being balanced with the needs of the individual mentee.

3. Political bias due to selfishness of the mentor to benefit from the capabilities of the mentee. This is one of the downsides of the concept of sponsorship.

Sponsorship

Throughout history, one form of mentorship that has dominated some cultures and organizations is sponsorship. Utilized historically and extensively in Chinese and Japanese cultures but also evident in the West, it is a process by which senior or important people in an organization become supporters of more junior individuals to help them with their career while they work for them.

Sylvia Ann Hewett describes the differences as follows:

"Mentors act as a sounding board or a shoulder to cry on, offering advice as needed and support and guidance as requested; they expect very little in return. Sponsors, in contrast, are much more vested in their protégés, offering guidance and critical feedback because they believe in them.

Sponsors advocate on their protégés' behalf, connecting them to important players and assignments. In doing so, they make themselves look good. And precisely because sponsors go out on a limb, they expect stellar performance and loyalty."

An oft-used example is Sheryl Sandberg, now COO of Facebook, who, while at the World Bank, was sponsored by Larry Summers who was the Chief Economist.

Hewett's research following 100 managers and almost 10,000 staff in the UK and United States from 2010 to 2012 indicated that a sponsorship arrangement led to a 30% increase in stretch assignments and gaining raises.

The theory behind sponsorship sounds fine when it encourages strong senior mentors to pluck highly capable mentees to their area of responsibility. And indeed, it may have value on that basis. However, it is not mentoring:

- It is a narrow and biased approach—for the few only. It is really a continuation of an elite form of high performer selection process that's evident historically in command-and-control systems.

- There is no evidence that this can be transformed into a wider system that can be integrated into a broader talent development approach.

- It is counter to the whole concept of mentoring, which is about the mentee being enabled to make their own decisions.

Conclusion

To summarize, internal mentoring has significant value:

- When organized well and integrated into a talent management system

- When the career interest of the mentee is primarily within that organization
- When mentoring is as devoid of internal politics as possible

II. The External Mentor

While individuals have often been informally mentored by individuals outside of their organization, in recent decades this opportunity has become more widely available and organized. The drivers have been:

- The need to access greater diversity of gender and ethnic background, experience, and perspective.

- The need to access greater diversity of experience across organizations within specific skills, e.g., accounting, IT, marketing, sales, etc.

- Less organization-specific "careering" with people moving jobs more frequently and therefore less organization-specific in their needs.

- A greater focus on networking and the role of the mentor in providing links and activities across people and organizations.

In this environment, groups offering not only well-matched mentor opportunities but also aid in the training and disciplines of mentoring, have arisen. There are hundreds available, addressing every gender, ethnicity, skill and age. Examples include these:

1. American Marketing Association Toronto (AMA Toronto) Mentor Exchange and Career Accelerator for marketing personnel (as described in Case #1.2)

2. Association of Fundraising Professionals (AFP) Mentorship Program

3. Big Brothers/Big Sisters Canadian Mentoring Partnership for youth

4. Canadian Women's Foundation (CWF) Go Girls Youth Program

5. Futurpreneur Canada for young entrepreneurs

6. Infection, Prevention and Control Canada (ipac/pci) Mentorship Program for staff in healthcare

7. NextGen Builders for professional trades people with recent focus on black youth

8. Project Management Institute (PMI) Mentoring Program

9 Toronto Region Immigrant Employment Council (TRIEC) Mentoring Partnership for immigrants

10. Women in Communications & Technology (WCT/FCT) National Mentorship Program

There has also been an evolution in the activity of these external groups. Many started with informal programs to help people meet mentors, like Ten Thousand Coffees. However, as the research developed and it was recognized that a more disciplined approach aided effectiveness, nearly all added additional services.

For example, here are AMA Toronto Mentor Exchange's additional services:

1. Has a "professional" mentor–mentee matching process

2. Has agreements with mentors and mentees that establish the program's length (one year) and meeting frequency and sends follow up communication to ensure it is occurring

3. Does a full evaluation amongst both mentors and mentees at the end of the year

4. Has training for both mentors and mentees in how to maximize value from mentoring sessions

5. Runs events covering topics in marketing delivered by mentors and other speakers enabling networking with other mentors and mentees in the program.

6. Recognizes mentorship contribution as part of the selection criteria for Canada's Marketing Hall of Legends inductees, and publicizes the winners.

In the post-pandemic era involvement in external programs has many advantages for mentors:

1. Enables exposure to areas of interest/development for the mentor outside of their current organization and its industry.

2. Broadens mentoring capability, and therefore, management capability.

3. Can provide true mentoring experience outside of any internal political issues.

4. Improves "presence" in the marketplace.

5. An added "give-back" contribution to the community.

Conclusion

In her presentations to the AMA Toronto Mentor Exchange mentors, Megan Mitchell talks about the importance for mentors to work on some of the 24-character strengths identified by the VIA Institute on Character. Based around characteristics of wisdom, courage, humanity, justice, temperance, and transcendence, these are then classified further to help mentor analysis of what aspects in the mentee can be developed to:

1. Amplify and grow the positive, and

2. Learn from and reframe the negative.

The point she makes is that the process of "nudging" a mentee's development is to achieve improvement and that is what makes a great mentor.

Whether part of an internal or external program, the ability to guide ("nudge") talent positively and productively without bureaucratic directives, to listen to viewpoints and input and by doing so to accomplish organizational goals, is now a key management capability for everyone. This is true now more than ever in a hierarchy-flattened, remote/collocated, blended, diverse organization with variable employment and increased needs for innovation to survive and compete. Two cases of mentor experience that follow reflect this.

Case #2.1. A Mentor's Perspective

Interview with Troy A. Sedgwick, Founder, President/CEO, Rec Media Inc., Calgary, for 26 years. Long-time mentor with AMA Toronto Mentor Exchange and recognized as "Mentor of the Year" in 2015. Sedgwick is also active in mentoring programs with Haskayne School of Business Mentorship Program at the University of Calgary and The Entrepreneurs Organization (EO).

A passionate believer in mentorship's benefits, Troy Sedgwick continues to be both a mentor and mentee. Indeed, one of his favourite phrases is "wise people seek the wise counsel of others" and he has followed that counsel from his earliest days. Troy sought his first mentor from within the marketing industry and had regular meetings. To this day, he continues to have two other people he considers mentors and seeks advice and counsel from them.

He became involved formally as a mentor with AMA Toronto Mentor Exchange, the Haskayne Mentorship Program, as well as EO for entrepreneurial start-ups.

It has been a most successful experience both for his mentees and himself. So what does he see as the founding principles for a good mentor–mentee relationship? *"Authenticity and vulnerability—being real."*

"... you find out that they [the mentor] are human beings. They have wisdom to share, mistakes they've made, and in a mentor relationship, if it is done right, the authenticity and vulnerability displayed by the mentor are really encouraging to the mentee. They realize it's okay to make mistakes, that failing is a big part of becoming a success and that you don't have to have it all figured out. Hearing that from a mentor can be inspiring as it was with my mentor relationship. That authenticity and vulnerability are key to any subject you are going to tackle, whether it is personal or professional."

To allow the mentee to feel comfortable discussing their own concerns, the mentor must be prepared to open themselves up.

Other guidelines that he sees as valuable include making the time for the mentee, however busy the mentor might be. The point is that there is always value. The mentor's honest reflections and "teaching moments" have huge value to the mentor as well as the mentee.

"Dispensing wisdom that I've garnered from others is like a mirror reflecting back on me and I think, I have not done that myself for a while!"

The meetings are therefore to Troy *"incredibly enriching, incredibly fulfilling, absolutely worth the time."*

In addition, Troy counsels against *"too much advice giving. Try not to give advice, but experience—share."* Allow the mentee to be smart enough to figure out how, and in what way, that experience applies to them. It reduces *"the defense mechanisms that go up when someone says, what you need to do is…."*

Troy does believe that some planning and preparation for mentor–mentee meetings is valuable, but he counsels at making the process too rigid:

"I have seen both ends of the spectrum. Mentorship programs that have just been 'here's your person, have fun'—no structure, no plan. And I've seen other programs that have gone too far—too many training courses, too much reading to do, too much structure. Some structure is needed: the regularity of meetings and the mentee to bring some challenges and issues for discussion. Otherwise, it becomes just a conversation about hockey or the weather."

Just in case, Troy brings some "meaty" questions himself based on previous discussions with the mentee and/or changes in the business environment.

He believes some training is valuable to ensure that ways to open up authentic discussion are enabled, but they should not become a rigid series of rules to be followed. The point is to have meetings with purpose but not ones that reduce spontaneity and inhibit an open discussion.

Troy sees value in specific subject area mentors and programs (like marketing), organization specific programs and general programs. The point is to meet the needs of the mentee and have them source whichever fit their needs at different points in their career.

He sees tremendous value in exposure to perspectives outside the focus of some programs or the linear experience of the mentor. This provides value in challenging too much silo-based thinking.

"Having someone outside your space is often where those real paradigm shifts happen. Work and life experience is valuable irrespective of which industries you've been in."

While the online world has advantages in terms of easing connections over distance, convenience, and engagement with people in the comfort of their home surroundings, Troy still misses face-to-face human connection, to be able to *"look people in the eyes as well as having a coffee or glass of wine."* As he says, the hospitality aspect is an important part of building the relationship.

However, video online mentoring sessions still have tremendous value: he rates face-to-face sessions at a high of 10, phone calls at a 3, and online video sessions as a 7/8. The point is that mentorship conversations done with authenticity are still of tremendous value in all forms.

When asked about the mentorship experience and contribution to his management style, he was immediately positive:

"Mentorship has made me a better manager too. Just learning, further refining how to interact with others, how to share openly and recognize that we are all students. I learn from my mentees as much as I do from my mentors. When I am interacting with my staff, I try to use the mentorship experience and become a teachable spirit for those who work for me."

He anticipates a further flattening of organizational hierarchies and, therefore, greater importance given to middle management and front line employees in their decision making. However, as he points out, this does not reduce the need for clear decision making. It requires leadership that involves:

".... collaboration, sometimes that humbling of yourself, that quelling of pride. But someone has to call the shots. Everybody must be heard, but someone still has the accountability for the decision."

To Troy, a mentor can be anyone with the right experience and attitude. He does agree that certain groups may need matches that reflect who they are by gender, religion, race, and background, but he hopes these also do not become silos of thought. Again humbleness, listening, authenticity, and vulnerability are the key characteristics for contribution whatever the cultural or other backgrounds of the mentor. The value of mentorship to the mentor is:

"When I have given my time in a mentoring relationship, I have received back by having the mirror turned on me and recognizing something I've neglected to do of late wherein my own life I could be better. Or just the satisfaction of having shared things I have learned over the years. It is incredibly rewarding, incredibly fulfilling—it's 'the sharpening of the saw.' I end up as a better business leader, a better father, family man, and a better human being."

Interview: February 19, 2021

Case #2.2. A Mentor's Perspective from an Internal Program and from Informal Relationships

Interview with Andrew Zimakas, currently Chief Product and Revenue Officer at Medcan. Previously CEO, Sprout Wellness Solutions; SVP Corporate Strategy, Loyalty One; SVP and Chief Marketing Officer, ING Direct, which became Tangerine Bank.

Andrew Zimakas's career had taken him from P&G to the technology space (with roles at Microsoft and AOL) and strategy consulting before his roles at Tangerine, Loyalty One, then Sprout, a startup in software services related to health and well-being. With this background he then was appointed to his current role at Medcan, a corporate wellness and executive health clinic. He had been mentored in the early roles, which had helped him understand the opportunities outside of the packaged goods business and provided guidance to him in his career and management practices.

At Tangerine he was part of their corporate mentorship program and had three mentees. They were a mixed group: one from IT, one from HR involved in change management, and one new millennial employee. Over time he continued his mentee relations as he successfully mentored his group with whom he has remained connected.

As he says, his involvement was:

"to give back based on my experience. But it was also very rewarding for me as there was a lot that I could learn too, be it related to the perspectives of millennial employees or advancements in technology."

Since leaving Tangerine, his mentorship experiences have been more informal, but he remains a passionate believer in the practice whether it is structured formally or informally and both in internal as well as external programs. Medcan for example does not currently have formal programs, but with its continued success may be considering one. In the interim, Andrew is drawing on his previous experience:

"As I was rebuilding my team and as we have grown that team, I've tried to initiate very spontaneous discussions to get the pulse of how things

are going. I expect many of these ongoing interactions will develop into a mentee relationship."

Andrew sees mentorship as a very contemporary leadership capability, which involves nudging people in a direction rather than just top-down orders. He sees this as particularly important in the management of millennials. The process adds leadership value to both mentors and mentees.

There are needs for both internal and external programs. Internal programs tend to have well defined goals and initiatives and a high level of commitment on both sides. However, the process could be too narrow to the organization, and its industry may become too political. External programs offer different and valuable perspectives, and in many ways, because they are outside of a specific job role, are often more personal.

"The external programs can have inherent value by being outside of any political or other conflicts that can arise despite the best of intentions. Additionally, having that external perspective has become more important than ever given how careers progress now. Career paths have typically become more varied, and people embrace more career-related changes than 20–30 years ago when I was starting out. The ideal is that you can blend the internal and external together even though it is more of a commitment."

The potential weaknesses of mentorship programs are that they are often less structured and disciplined in approach and thus there may be less commitment by participants. Peer mentoring can also be effective though too often it is too informal and social.

Mentorship often involves a blend of both mentoring—which is more mentee-focused and typically a broader engagement—and coaching, which tends to be more prescriptive.

Not every session will have value, but over time it can help the mentee in three areas: one's job/role, personal values, and home life.

The mentor's role is to bring a broader perspective and to aid and nudge the mentee in their own decision-making. Andrew believes mentors should not seek to pass judgement or craft others in their own image. Rather, they should help the mentee see different opportunities, broaden their perspective on career matters, get outside of the day-to-day pressures, and build confidence in the mentee's own decision-making. Listen and nudge, not talk and direct.

"Enlighten them on certain options, help 'open the aperture,' but in the end it is really the mentee who must make the decisions."

The mentee role is to approach the sessions with goals to be accomplished and to ensure regular engagement. They should be receptive and look for connection points between ideas, advice, and contacts.

In Andrew's view mentees don't necessarily require directly matched backgrounds with their mentors. Rather, they should be clear about their goals and what they want from the relationship in terms of interest and values.

These relationships, in his view, can and should be developed over time:

"It is incumbent on the mentee to gain value by maintaining relationships, both formally within the program, but also to take the initiative to stay in touch after the formal relationship has ended and extend it into a deeper relationship for the balance of their career."

In terms of the changes Andrew has seen, one of the biggest is in the mentor–mentee exchange:

"Over the last few years I see more of the 'reverse mentoring' dynamic taking place. While I have accumulated additional experience to give, there is so much that is now coming back to me in the relationships. It is really a value exchange, and I don't mean that in the transactional way, but a really meaningful mutual exchange."

While Andrew prefers face-to-face sessions, everyone has learned to cope with virtual communication. While not ideal, he senses at Medcan some positives:

"There is a feeling that we are all in this together. It's okay to let people into what they are struggling with. Sometimes it is with humour, other times it's a little more serious, but I think there is more of a sense of shared experience. I do wonder that coming into the office is rather like putting on your work 'body armour.' It sends a message that this is your work-self, which is different from your home-self, and never the two shall meet. A

lot of that has gone out the window and there is now a little more genuine presentation of who we are. This is not only more refreshing but arguably a more productive way of approaching work."

Medcan, being a "wellness" organization, has given a lot of thought to the post-pandemic pattern of working: they *"have had their eyes opened"* to a lot of possibilities including a more flexible hybrid model of work:

"It involves bringing back people to the office—whether it's on designated days or in a less structured way—and combining that with time away to 'think/do'; while the in-office element is very much centred on collaboration: getting together, working through things, and if appropriate, making decisions together. I think that can be a highly effective model."

In summary, Andrew sees mentorship as a key part of this emerging future:

"It reinforces consideration of people as the organization's greatest asset and actively encourages that 'value exchange' we talked about earlier. Within a company it is a process whereby the mentee can tap into the mentor's career track record and experience inside and outside the organization including the corporate knowledge and corporate memory. It can also reinforce the feeling of belonging and confidence that can be engendered for the mentee. You then layer on the 'reverse mentoring' component, the 'value exchange' that flows in the direction of the mentor, which provides the opportunity for later career engagement, revitalization, and that opportunity to give back."

Interviews conducted February 26, 2021, and May 2015

3

BEING A GREAT MENTEE

"Courage is what it takes to stand up and speak. Courage is also what it takes to sit down and listen."

— Winston Churchill, 1874–1965, former UK Prime Minister

While to some it may seem that the weight of responsibility of a great mentoring relationship lies with its organization and the mentor, this is not true. The success of a mentoring relationship actually lies with the mentee. The whole point about mentoring is that the mentee must take responsibility for their development and therefore the mentoring. This principle applies throughout the whole process: from seeking the right combination of organizations delivering the mentorship program (internal and/or external), to establishing the matching criteria and accepting the mentor, to organizing the mentor–mentee process (topics, meeting length, meeting frequency, balance of formal to informal sessions, and career versus personal issues), and to the evaluation of the success and longevity of the relationship.

There is general agreement and research support that a mentoring relationship needs to have the following characteristics.

Characteristics of a Great Mentoring Relationship

- Collaboration: mentee and mentor play a partnership role
- Communication: open and honest so that both can share strengths and weaknesses; dreams and goals; past, present and anticipated experiences
- Confidentiality: all conversations held are totally confidential and in a safe space.; this is particularly important in internal mentoring
- Joint accountability: to build trust mentee and mentor must keep agreements, timing and promises
- Respect: mutual appreciation of the knowledge and investment of time, energy, and wisdom
- Responsiveness: both mentor and mentee need to be sensitive and responsive to the goals, needs and especially perspectives of the other

While all parties to the mentorship need to attend to these, the role of the mentee is essential for success.

What the Mentee Must Bring to the Relationship

- Know yourself: be honest with yourself about who you are, where you are in your career and job, what you think you are capable of, and what you may not be.

- Set goals: what do you want to attain from the relationship: short, medium, long term? Remember, the goals can/should be both IQ- and EQ-based—knowledge of and how your personality uses that knowledge with others: self-awareness and social awareness. If career goals, how much is internal, and how much should be general professional or managerial.

- Review the matching criteria: be sure the mentor has the experience and values that are important to your needs.

- Take an active role in building the relationship: be proactive; initiate contact when needed (but don't abuse their time); and, most of all, follow through with agreements.

- Be prepared: do your research and always come to meetings with your own thoughts or solutions to your issues.

- Share honestly: tell your mentor what is really on your mind and what you want from the relationship and in your career, to try something different, to look at some things differently. Be curious and exploratory. Talk about your future and the mentor's past.

- Try to resist being threatened by feedback and criticism: use it to support yourself in your learning. Use it to open up opportunities that push you.

- Ask questions and listen carefully to the answers: don't assume your mentor's views are the same as yours. Listen and consider.

- Keep a record of key learning: it does not need to be elaborate, but a written record will aid your reflection.

- Make time to reflect on the conversation: sometimes it can make a great topic for the next session with your mentor.

- Set next steps for both any actions you are to take, and future conversations.

- Show appreciation for your mentor's engagement—not financially but through thanks and contributions to their learning and networking.

- Enjoy the process, have fun, and enjoy the conversations.

So how should the process work?

Mentee Process

1. Be consistent with the first two points in the previous section. The mentee should be clear about what they want out of a mentor relationship: self-analysis to determine what type of mentor and mentoring, and what they want from the relationship.

2. Search existing mentorship programs: both internal and external. See which seems to fit your needs best. You can choose two, but be prepared to put in a considerable amount of time and effort. If it is your first experience, choose only one.

3. At the same time as you are reviewing mentorship programs, review the mentor matching process: does it contain the criteria that would be relevant to what you have decided in number 1? If you don't have an internal program or don't find what you want in a search of external programs, decide on the kind of mentor you

want and search your networks and contacts for someone suitable. Use "Ten Thousand Coffees" to start the process.

4. If it is an internal program, review the political issues and decide how you will manage the opportunities this provides.

5. At your first mentor meeting, discuss what you want out of the relationship; discuss each other's backgrounds and set an agenda and timetable.

6. Decide how you want to proceed for future meetings:

    - How often

    - Length

    - Content

    - Format: in-person, phone, Skype/Zoom

    However, where possible in the mentorship system with which you are engaged, build in room for non-scheduled meetings for informal discussions.

7. Think about an agenda for your meetings. Our preference is that it should be written and sent to the mentor ahead of time. In this way you should cover all issues and enable the mentor to have thinking and reflection time.

8. Make notes after the meetings so that you have reference material for later reflection.

9. Set up a review session on how things are going. You decide when based on your frequency of contact. Three months? Six months?

10. When moving on, agree to have future contacts and discuss the next phase in your experience: to have another mentee relationship or maybe to become a mentor.

Conclusion

The point about the mentorship process in the contemporary environment, and especially in marketing, is that there is always a need to learn from others and a need for you to help develop others. Remember that old expression: that the best way to understand a concept is to explain it to someone else. Or in the words of an ancient Roman philosopher:

"While we teach, we learn."

— Seneca, c.4BCE–65AD, Roman philosopher

The stories from two mentees that follow vividly illustrate not only value to the mentee but to their mentors and the organization in general. Mentoring is always of two-way value and also of organizational value, especially in the post-pandemic world.

Case #3.1. A Mentee's Perspective

Interview with Anjum Sultana, Manager Service Quality and Process Improvement – Planning and Engineering, Federal Express Canada (FedEx). With a highly successful ten-year career with FedEx following her first job in Canada with Microsoft and her immigration from Pakistan, Anjum has had mentee experience at FedEx and at the AMA Toronto Mentor Exchange where in 2018 she was voted "Mentee of the Year."

Brought up and educated with an MBA along with doing work as a senior media planner in a media agency in Karachi, Sindh Province, Pakistan, Anjum made the bold move to Canada in her early 20s. Following work with Microsoft, she has pursued a career with a company she loves, FedEx Canada.

"The thing I know about FedEx is that it really is a people company. They hired me for my potential and have taken me to different places: I am now in my seventh role. It has been exciting. It is the most family, non-family company."

As a very energetic, smart, and learning-oriented individual, Anjum sought mentors through her career, albeit mostly informally. Her first formal mentorship program was when FedEx recommended her for the "Women's Executive Network" where she had Nancy Marcus as her mentor. That really got Anjum interested in continuing a more formal mentor relationship.

She views the mentor–mentee relationship as different based on the personalities, but always includes:

"… acting as a 'sounding board', describing my situation and asking 'what would you do given your experience—here's what I think I want to do, how would you approach it?"

With her AMA Toronto Mentor Exchange mentor, Andrea Graham, the relationship has been exceptionally close:

"The relationship has been seamless; it is very clear what I expect of her and she expects of me. It just feels like we've known each other for so long."

Agenda-setting for their discussions was different between her mentors: with Nancy it was a little more planned and formal; with Andrea, more fluid but always set in advance. Anjum's goals were usually to help her navigate her career at FedEx but over time changed, matured:

"... it became more about the longer term, what kind of a leader I want to be. More of the 'soft skills'."

Mentoring conversations were not always about *"work work"* but rather *"evolving as a person."*

As Anjum sees it, this characteristic of the relationship was due to the close chemistry that she and Andrea developed. As she commented, the mentor–mentee relationship does vary with the personalities and their "fit" together.

Key success factors in the mentor–mentee relationship for Anjum were:

- Making sure it is really a two-way conversation.

- Making sure the conversation is open and honest so that trust is built.

- Having the mentor understand and put themselves in the mentee's situation.

- Being sure that the issues are discussed thoroughly. Or to quote Anjum, "The difference between having a valuable conversation and a cursory conversation."

- For the mentee to respect the time the mentor is spending.

- If necessary, being flexible with both timing and content of the conversation to accommodate other occasional pressures from work and home.

- Allowing the relationship to grow.

- Even changing mentors at different work/life stages, and therefore needs, of the mentee.

- Anjum has no problem with different backgrounds for mentorship (which was her experience at FedEx): gender, race, religion, or indeed work experience. In fact, she likes learning from people with different work experiences, as it helps broaden her perspective.

She sees different strengths and weaknesses between internal company programs and external programs:

"The strength of internal is that they understand the political landscape better—especially with a global company like FedEx. And also somebody who really understands 'where you sit' within the company, whether it is how you are perceived or what are some of the things you want to improve in that perception of the company."

For external programs:

"What gave me a little more confidence is 'street credit'. What I am doing is not just valuable internally but also 'on the street'. This would give me the confidence to know that I'm on the right track in my career choices."

As far as the coaching vs. mentoring discussion is concerned, she thinks there are times for both. Sometimes a little more directed coaching, other times more questioning, nudging, and encouraging self-discovery. It has to evolve with the specific mentor–mentee relationship.

"Sometimes I wish the mentor would tell me that in my situation, this is what they would do. But my confidence is that with the right amount of pushing, I would come to that conclusion myself."

Anjum absolutely understands that she has taught her mentors some things: *"for instance, the newer ways of conducting things in the digital landscape and so on."*

Indeed, as Anjum moves into her own mentor roles at FedEx, she reflects, based on her experience:

"How would I shape things with a person so that we can be open, transparent, and honest so that we have valuable conversations and that trust and respect are there. The key is how you get people to do certain things because they want to do them. With one person I have mentored, I knew she was wanting to do something but needed the push and the comfort to actually do it, which, by the way, she did and brilliantly."

The value of mentoring for Anjum will continue. As she says:

I am an 'A' type personality, and I will always value getting the softer side right so that people don't feel intimidated and, instead, I can bring them along."

In Anjum's view mentoring requires from the mentee:

"You've got to be open to listening to the good, the bad, and the ugly about yourself."

And the value is:

"to find a connection with someone at work or in your immediate community, or someone with a more senior role and perspective."

For Anjum Sultana:

"It's benefited me a lot; it's made a substantial difference in my understanding of myself, in how I present myself, how people perceive me, and that's been really beneficial."

Interview: February 23, 2021

Case #3.2. Mentee becomes Mentor

Interview with Mike Muyal, currently General Manager, LEVOLOR Canada, a Hunter Douglas company, following Director of Marketing positions with them, and a career with Newell Brands, Unilever and Revlon amongst others. Mentee and then Mentor experience with AMA Toronto Mentor Exchange and the Rotman School of Business Marketing Association mentorship program.

Throughout his education, especially at the John Molson School of Business at Concordia University and McGill, and in his early work life, Mike Muyal had mentoring relationships—albeit informal—that he fondly remembers:

"Peers at work and people at a higher level would help me navigate corporate culture, but also professors who were people I could lean on and went the extra mile for me. Many really inspired me."

These all helped his learning through more of a dialogue than formal teaching or coaching, which led him later to seek more formal programs.

He first got involved in a formal mentorship program with the AMA Toronto Mentor Exchange as a mentee to:

"... broaden my horizons and get a better perspective on marketing in the Toronto community."

Becoming a mentee, Mike had clear goals that he carried forward when he became a mentor:

"... the learning and the ability to exchange ideas. Not so much networking ideas or job opportunities, but more for ideas about their perspective on the business world—different types of businesses and industries, and how they worked and how they functioned. That thirst for knowledge is what I then brought forward as a mentor along with the friendship and the camaraderie and willingness to listen that had developed with my mentor."

The other motivations for Mike in the transition from mentee to mentor were wanting to "give back" and to become a better hiring and general manager:

"I said to myself, I want to be the kind of person like my mentor was to me, to somebody else. Learning about the kind of experiences, the struggles and perspective so that I could help someone looking for a job or developing their career."

Like other good mentors, Mike did not want to force any agenda on his mentees; he wanted an open book conversation—rather like his general management style. He was available to talk about anything the mentee wanted, both personal life and business life, as they always overlapped. He wanted to hear the mentee point of view and then add his own perspective from his experience:

"being clear that the viewpoint is my point of view and not necessarily the 'right' one—keeping an open mind."

Other guidelines Mike took to the mentee–mentor transition were to be available when that person needed the conversation and also in the form of the meeting: although Mike preferred in-person meetings, sometimes phone conversations were appropriate and in the pandemic period video meetings took over.

In the mentor relationship, Mike's mentees wanted to understand his industry background and views—not surprising given his long successful career in both sales and marketing in the fashion industry (Helene Curtis, Schwarzkopf, and Revlon); packaged goods (Unilever); and the home goods industry (Newell Brands and LEVOLOR).

The other conversations were, as Mike put it:

"wanting to understand who we are as people. So, I would get questions about managing work and family life."

During the pandemic, working with both his mentees and company staff, he has become much more engaged in the overlap between home life and work life. The more open conversations Mike has had with his mentees have helped him with his own staff: sharing personal and work life together.

He sees coaching as important but a bit narrower than mentoring:

"Mentoring is a bit broader, a little longer-term, less with any real set agenda. Coaching can help you with public speaking, for example, but mentoring helps you understand its role and context."

In reflecting on internal and external mentorship programs he sees advantages and disadvantages with both and therefore a need for both:

"Internal programs can address many of the challenges that a mentee can have within the scope of that company. Communicating what those challenges are—political, behavioural, understanding the system—and how to overcome them can be handled better by the internal programs.

"The advantages of doing it externally are that it will be a little more impartial and unbiased, with more focus on the personal relationship factor. These programs may also be less forced, as they are voluntary whereas internal programs could be seen as a little 'forced' as part of company policy—too much 'let's check the box'."

Matches of mentor and mentee need not always be siloed. Depending on mentee needs, in his view it will often be valuable to have a finance mentee aligned with a marketing mentor.

"There is always something to learn whoever you are with."

Indeed, he absolutely believes this continues throughout your life, however senior you become. Mike himself has a mentor in the United States at the Atlanta office of LEVOLOR. He has also had a mentor relationship with a vendor organization executive: in Mike's case it was a PR agency executive.

Mentor–mentee relationships can be exhausted and change at different career stages, but they can morph into an ongoing mutually supportive relationship where each mentor and mentee continually guides the other.

The key for success lies in the depth of the relationship. As Mike puts it:

"….be sensitive to what the mentee seems to be asking for; the words may come out in a certain way—like job hunting or enquiring about different industries—but it may not be that. Probe, ask, tell them don't be shy; find out what's behind the question. Search and don't be afraid to dig deep. Go back into your past, expose yourself because you will be seen as genuine and that will help your mentee discuss what's really on their mind."

Interview: February 25, 2021

4

NEW DIRECTIONS IN MENTORING

"Tell me and I forget. Teach me and I may remember. Involve me and I learn."

— Benjamin Franklin, 1705–1790, American writer, political philosopher, scientist, statesman

Since the Mentor Exchange started in 2010, and as mentoring's role in management has become more important, new versions have arisen. While still primarily viewed as an individual–individual relationship, it now has many variations. We have already discussed informal and formal mentoring as well as internal and external matters; others that have developed include:

Self-mentoring

Frankly, the author is not keen on this. Mentorship is an invaluable process of exchanging, listening, thinking, discussion, and decision. However, some works do indicate the value of a disciplined self-improvement process. Joseph Graham, for example, recommends a six-sequence of self-knowledge: context (what is happening around you); scaling (seeing patterns, risks, and risk mitigation); flow (logistics planning); spiral based thinking (integration of activity); and the role of artificial intelligence. However good this approach is or may be, the author believes strongly that in a social world understanding how the self develops and contributes is hugely aided by others in exploration and discussion.

Reverse-mentoring

Seniority in role/title, while still a factor, is no longer as important: it is seniority and exposure in experience that has become more important. As such one of the developments is so-called "reverse-mentoring."

With changes in technology and human behaviour, it is often the person more junior in age who has the greater knowledge and experience. We see this particularly in marketing with the emergence of ever new technologies, applications, and habits in communication.

Positioning new capabilities in the context of older ones is still important: that is why mentoring is a two-way process.

Some corporations have recognized the value of this approach: IBM and P&G are famous examples. One of the most famous was General Electric under its then CEO Jack Welch, who required 500 of their top managers to find employees well versed in the technology of the Internet and tap into that expertise. In the book about IBM practices, *Intelligent Mentoring*, three huge advantages are cited:

- It defines the nature of mentoring relationships by expertise, not by title or status within the organization.

- It makes the exchange of knowledge and resources a shared enterprise.

- It transforms relationships from being primarily a tool to gain technical expertise into a vehicle for learning.

Reciprocal Mentoring

Two people agree to a "mentoring partnership" and take turns in mentoring each other as peers. The disciplines described earlier still apply to ensure it becomes more than just an enjoyable conversation. The advantage is in often "safe space" sharing of questions, answers, listening, and reflection.

eMentoring/Virtual Mentoring

One of the impacts of the pandemic that will continue afterward is the greater use of technology to enable communication from many locations. Use of phones has been massively improved by video-based meetings enabled by services like Zoom, Skype, GoToMeeting, Slack, Google Meet, Cisco Webex, Microsoft Teams, Bluejeans, Join.me, BigBlueButton, and Blackboard Collaborate.

The principles of mentorship still apply whether the use is exclusive or mixed with in-person events. Mentors and mentees have to determine what blend they feel most comfortable with. If it is totally online, then different methods to improve engagement should be tried. Use of online learning methods could be helpful: encouraging storytelling, trade-off questions, assignments, etc.

In fact, in the summer of 2020 at one AMA Toronto Mentor–Mentee Zoom meeting, many commented how close mentor–mentee relationships had become, because instead of just an in-person at-work context, people saw home accommodation, families, and pets, and so they understood each other as persons rather than just roles.

There are, however, challenges with virtual mentoring. In the area of youth mentoring isolation has proved a growing problem during the pandemic. As such, some professionals, like Michael Garringer, Director of Research and Evaluation at MENTOR: The National Mentoring Partnership, noted the creation of virtual mentoring portals that help volunteers maintain relationships with youth:

> *"In the face of the significant barriers posed by social distancing, many mentors have kept their eye on the prize by staying connected in whatever ways they can, whether through video calling, social media and other web-based interactive platforms, drive-bys, drop-offs of care packages and notes and even good old-fashioned letters."*

These contact additions to all target groups during virtual mentoring can also help offset feelings of isolation or lack of interest. As noted in the IBM Case (4.3) IBM has now established an internal portal that can be used for such contact with its own staff.

Group Mentoring

Given changes caused by the effects of the pandemic and the accelerated use of technology, we expect this method to increase significantly. It also connects with the very changes described as necessary to improve performance in *Humanocracy* earlier.

In its simplest terms, group mentoring involves one mentor meeting with several mentees at the same time. The mentor poses questions, listens, draws all mentees into the conversation, reflects and feeds back.

Historically, variations of this approach can be seen in two forms:

- Mastermind groups: think tanks described by Napoleon Hill in Ann Rolfe's work as: "...*a group of brains, co-ordinated (or connected) in a spirit of harmony, will provide more thought energy than a single brain, just as a group of electric batteries will provide more energy than a single battery...the increased energy created by that alliance becomes available to every brain in the group.*"

- Mentoring circles: elements of peer mentoring and mastermind groups. In his *Harvard Business Review* article, "Our Work-from-Anywhere Future," Prithwiraj Choudhury describes cases of "temporary collection events" and "remote communities of practice" where this kind of event takes place to add connection for people working from different locations. The thought of building these connections is important, but it lacks the discipline of mentor relations.

Given changes in organization design and process described earlier, we expect the Group Mentoring model to develop further. KMP in Europe has already worked in this arena.

KMP suggest the following:

- The most common form consists of one to two mentors with a group of five to ten mentees collaborating around learning and sharing.

- The mentees share a broad learning goal.

- Members are responsible for their own learning and for that of the others in the group.

- All meet at the same time and discuss the same topic.

- Mentors are the learning partners and facilitators for the group.

- The process is a combination of group facilitation and peer mentoring.

The following advantages are evident:

- Mentees gain insights from both mentors and peers.

- Sharing in a group generates a sense of teamwork.

- With the number of people in the group, greater diversity of thinking, practice, and understanding can be achieved.

- By forming groups from across organizational silos, greater coherence of solutions and action can be achieved.

- Use of these groups with good mentorship in everyday management can reduce bureaucratic levels that cost more and can slow organizational response and stifle innovation.

- Use of these groups in everyday management can improve the "humanity" of the work environment.

Relative to more individualized mentoring, there are some disadvantages, which mean a combination of forms is often beneficial. The disadvantages are:

- The process is less personal, and the level of confidentiality may be limited.

- Competition for the mentor's attention could cause friction in the group rather than cooperation.

- Each mentee's different needs may not get accommodated.

- Meeting scheduling may be more complex.

We see tremendous advantages with group mentoring in marketing where individual specializations often get in the way of well-designed and coordinated activity.

In addition, the group application is well suited to cultures that are less individualistic in their values. Using Hofstede's individualism versus collectivism index, where a high score out of 100 means a more individualistic culture while a low score indicates a greater collectivism/group orientation, the group approach may work better in some countries or with some ethnic groups rather than others. Here are the contrasts:

- Although Canada is an individualistic culture (80), it is much less so than either the United States (91) or the UK (89) and closer to France (71) and Ireland (70)

- Countries that send immigrants to Canada in large numbers have much lower individualism indexes: here are examples based on Canada's immigration patterns:

India	48
Iran	41
Jamaica	39
Brazil	38
Philippines	32
Mexico	30
China–Hong Kong	25
China (mainland)	20

As such there is room for many types of mentoring approaches—individual and group. However, depending on the culture of the participants the balance of these may vary. More community-based cultures, both domestically and internationally, may experience greater effectiveness with group-based approaches. However, recognition of the power of a more individualistic mentor–mentee approach will still prove the most valuable.

Conclusion

There are many versions of mentorship processes being tried. Behind all of them is the concept of learning from experience but encouraging new thinking and interpretation of that experience based on fresh knowledge. The three cases that follow illustrate alternative corporate approaches to achieving this balance.

Case #4.1. An Internal Mentorship Program: Shopify Inc. Engineering Mentorship Program

Shopify Inc. is a 15-year-old, Cdn$2.929.5 million revenue (2020 fiscal year) Canadian multinational founded in Ottawa. It is a commerce company providing proprietary software platforms for online stores and retail point-of-sale systems serving approximately 1.7 million merchants. Shopify runs mentorship programs on a department-by-department basis. The Engineering Mentorship Program was put in place in 2020 and is run by Sarah and her team.

Interview with Sarah Naqvi, Senior Technical Education Program Manager, R&D Learning, Shopify Inc.

Sarah's background is an impressive mix of Computer Science Software Engineering (H.BSc. University of Toronto, teaching at UOIT, software development at IBM); Research (Institute of Child Study U. of T.); and Education (MA Child Study and Education at U. of T.; a K-8 teacher at the TDSB). For the last five years she has been at Shopify: firstly, as Computer Science Education Program Developer then for the last 3.5 years as Senior Technical Education Program Manager, R&D Learning.

Sarah works with Shopify technical employees, developers, designers, and scientists to help them find the best resources and the best way to learn, grow, and develop in their careers. This includes programs like its Engineering Mentorship Program.

Mentorship is deep in Sarah's personal career:

"Mentorship has always been a huge part of my life. I have always sought out mentors in my career and personal life. I've always valued having different perspectives. A great way to get where you want to go is to learn from people who have gotten there. I also try to be a mentor whenever I can help."

To Sarah:

"Mentorship is definitely a two-way street: a very reciprocal relationship. It provides guidance to help people reach their goals or explore a space that is maybe unknown: to hear about what you don't know and don't

know what questions to ask. For the mentor it is the opportunity to further develop their teaching/coaching/mentorship skills to help someone answer the questions for themselves. It is probing, listening and asking the right questions."

Before Sarah and her team set up the formal program in engineering, Shopify had many creative ways to encourage sharing of ideas: pairing programs to enable one-on-one peer meetings, for example. Shopify has been very intentional in encouraging people to connect, learn from each other and build relationships.

The first step in designing the Engineering Mentorship Program was research:

"We started exploring to get to know our engineers a little better rather than just apply general ideas from the industry. We researched and got to know our developers and engineers. We discovered they loved to learn from one another much more so than relying on a book or external peers. They saw each other as a trusted source. We discovered how really, really busy they were and had minimal time for dedicated learning. We also learned that they really did want to develop technically and in their leadership skills."

The program that resulted and launched just over a year earlier, runs in six-week cycles for a match of about 100 mentees with 100 mentors. At the time of talking to Sarah, they were on their fourth iteration.

Every two months engineers and developers have a chance to sign up either as a mentor or mentee or both. They fill in a sign-up form that indicates what areas they are interested in:

"Topics of interest, back-end/ front-end focus, management, new areas, or areas where they would like to be more supported. Then there's a matching process done online to pre-set questions."

The call for mentors emphasizes the value to them:

"We make it very clear that this is an opportunity for them to develop their leadership, coaching, and supporting another person's skills, and that is very much encouraged at Shopify."

In addition, there is a closed community for mentors so that they can exchange ideas and seek help about dealing with their mentees. Sarah sees this as an important part of the process.

Then there is the online mentor–mentee matching session based on the sign-in form responses. As far as possible they avoid having to make manual adjustments. As criteria they include:

"Making sure the mentor is not the mentee's manager. That the mentor and mentee are not on the same team. That there are areas of common interest based on the sign-up forms: there are about ten or so categories on the form that can be identified. Additionally, that the mentee's job level is less than or equal to the mentor."

There is then a kick-off session, and the mentors and mentees agree to meet each week for the next six weeks. The mentees set goals for the sessions, and the mentor helps, and part of the report back is the success in meeting those goals—though this is not a rigid measure:

"It's a moving target, something that they work towards."

Inclusion of this goal setting was added after the first iteration, and they have found that the satisfaction levels have improved since that addition.

At the end of each cycle an assessment is conducted. Success of the program is measured by responses to questions such as "Would you recommend the program?", and "Would you participate again?" The team will track the growth in the mentee's skills and confidence shown by the mentee in identifying their own skill gaps. Among the mentors, it is whether or not they feel it is improving their leadership skills. Sarah's team also plans to begin analyzing how many mentees return as mentors or for more mentee sessions.

Attendees are from every level at Shopify: newcomers as well as 10-year veterans and directors. Most matched relationships have worked well. Indeed, several mentee–mentor relationships have continued after the six-week session.

"At Shopify, because of our rate of growth and hiring, this intensive and extensive program has proved really important."

To guide the whole program, Sarah and her team created a Shopify Engineering Mentorship Guidebook to help both mentors and mentees optimize the value of the experience.

Sarah is a fan of all types of mentorship programs including external ones:

"I think we can all learn from others—it encourages an 'open mindset'. At Shopify we seize any opportunities to learn from the broader community: to bring back that knowledge and share that knowledge with the broader company."

Based on her personal experience, and the results of the Shopify Engineering Mentorship Program, Sarah is an enthusiastic advocate of mentorship as part of contemporary management practice:

"I honestly think mentorship programs are a great asset to any and every organization. They require such a small investment in them while their impact can be massive across the organization. Mentees develop craft skills. Mentors develop leadership and coaching skills. Both parties gain a broad understanding about the company, and learn and build relationships across work roles.

At Shopify we talk about being 'T shaped': a deep skill and expertise in a particular area, and the upper bar of the 'T' being where you build a broader scope and, while not being an expert, a broader lens on the business. You gain contact with other departments, skills, what they are working on, what they are learning and thinking. Individuals are then not just focused exclusively on what they know and do but get a better sense of where the company is going which can inform the work we are doing every day. It takes people's blinders off. I believe that is an asset to any organization."

In summary, Sarah sees mentorship in internal programs as combining different levels of experience and skills to enable people in the organization:

"To be able to have conversations, to share an idea that can have an impact on the organization. This is such a beautiful thing to help people and organizations to thrive at this unique time. While different organizations may need to 'tweak' their process to fit their culture, the underlying value is there for all."

Interview: March 4, 2021

Case #4.2. An Internal–External Mentorship Program: The Scotiabank Women Initiative.

Interview with Nicole German, VP & Global Head, Enterprise Digital Marketing, Sales & Growth, Scotiabank. In March 2021 Nicole added the responsibility of VP of The Scotiabank Women Initiative,TM having been an Advisory Board Member for two years.

Scotiabank is a leading bank in the Americas. Guided by their purpose "for every future," they help their customers, their families, and their communities achieve success through a broad range of advice, products, and services, including personal and commercial banking, wealth management and private banking, corporate and investment banking, and capital markets. Scotiabank has a team of approximately 90,000 employees and assets of approximately $1.2 trillion (as at January 31, 2021). Scotiabank launched "The Scotiabank Women Initiative" in December 2018 in support of women-led and women-owned businesses. Since then, it has scaled to support and help clients drive positive change in their careers and organizations and to empower women to take control of their financial futures.

Nicole German's career has included roles in Canada, Europe, and Latin America. She was appointed to her current global and digital role at Scotiabank in 2017, and in March 2021 added the responsibility of Vice President for "The Scotiabank Women Initiative" ("Initiative"). Prior to joining Scotiabank, she had a highly successful career in the technology and software world in both marketing and business development. She is an active leader in the not-for-profit space, and is Founder and Executive Director of The Maddie Project, a youth-oriented mental health not-for-profit organization. Her experience includes work with SAP, LinkedIn, Platform Computing (IBM), and advisory and director roles with PieSync (HubSpot) in Belgium, Talentoday (France), MaRS, and DMZ.

Recognizing the often unique challenges that women-led businesses face, the mission of the "Initiative" is to provide a comprehensive program to break down barriers to economic opportunity and to empower women to be in control of their financial futures through three pillars: access to capital and tailored financial solutions, education, and advice and mentorship.

In discussing the background to the establishment of the "Initiative" Nicole indicated:

"What we learned in our research is that there is an inherent unconscious bias that affects women in business and their ability to access financing. The program was started by Gillian Riley* after hearing directly from clients about the challenges that women in business were experiencing. The Scotiabank Women Initiative was founded in Scotiabank's Business Banking arm with a focus on women-led small businesses but also large organizations where women were on the executive leadership team. Then over the two years we evolved from primarily business support in Business Banking into supporting our women clients' careers and businesses in Global Banking and Markets, and then providing tailored wealth advisory services in Scotia Wealth Management."

*Gillian Riley is currently President & CEO, Tangerine Bank and executive sponsor of The Scotiabank Women Initiative. In 2018 she was Executive Vice President Scotiabank Canadian Commercial Banking.

The original program was founded on three pillars:

- Access to capital

- Access to mentorship

- Access to education

Shortly after its original launch, the "Initiative" made a clear commitment related to access to capital for women-led businesses: to deploy $3 billion over three years to fund women's businesses. It has since deployed over two-thirds of that commitment.

The two additional pillars were equally important:

"Providing women with mentorship and support is incredibly important. To provide a community, an ecosystem of support, as well as education depending on what their needs are. Initially that support system was about scaling and growing; recently it has been about how to pivot while addressing those needs."

Building on its initial success, Scotiabank extended the "Initiative" to its Global Banking and Markets business. Based on feedback received from women clients about the challenges they were facing in their careers, the team developed a comprehensive, tailor-made program for women clients—and the leaders and companies who stand behind an inclusion agenda—to take their careers and businesses even further. This program is also focused on three pillars—innovation, advisory, and education—designed to help women pursue their best professional futures. As part of a breadth of offerings, The Scotiabank Women Initiative for Global Banking and Markets offers women executives a Board governance program to prepare them to sit on Boards.

The most recent expansion came in 2020 with a bespoke wealth advisory program that builds on the foundation of Scotia's Total Wealth offering which focuses on transforming the way women clients are served.

"A lot of the transfer of wealth in the next few years will not only be generation to generation, but male to female. We wanted to help women be more confident in making financial decisions. Too often they have not been in the forefront of the conversation."

Initially the focus of the "Initiative" was on Scotiabank customers in the Canadian market, but it has evolved to a more global reach and non-Scotiabank customers can engage, though there remain some services specifically for current customers.

The effective delivery and promotion of "The Scotiabank Women Initiative" programming across Business Banking, Global Banking and Markets and Scotia Wealth Management required training and focus on Scotiabank's own staff and advisors in how they relate to women clients. It is not only about providing the right information to clients, but also ensuring that they are an active part of the conversation and are feeling empowered.

As such, there is a focus on building awareness and connections with and via Scotiabank's own employees:

"Our front-line teams and branch staff were briefed first about what the program is, what it can offer and how to assess the customer's interest and needs. The entire success of The Scotiabank Women Initiative has been led by a grass roots approach through our teams and our clients."

Supporting the on-the-ground Scotiabank staff is a well-developed web site and digital capability. In the bank's Knowledge Centre there is access to podcasts created by outside speakers (such as Shopify executives discussing the digital world): Inspiring Stories of successful women-run businesses, networking announcements and opportunities, and the bank's Learning Aids. Among the learning aids is an online session on "High Impact Mentoring" where the speakers from the Telfer School of Management at the University of Ottawa run through different mentorship styles and their strengths and weaknesses.

The Scotiabank Women Initiative has also connected with some outside groups who focus on women: both venture capital organizations and other organizations, as they fit the needs of the three pillars. Additionally, there is liaison with another Scotiabank program, a social impact program called ScotiaRise, which helps foster economic inclusion and resilience among disadvantaged groups. This can include women coming through the education process as well as women coming to Canada and the immigrant experience. In Nicole's view this combination provides a comprehensive program:

"... a force for growth and a force for good."

Nicole and her team are researching expansion of the "Initiative" into areas where women are even more challenged: indigenous groups, disabled communities, the LGBTQ community, and others.

"The mentorship and programming may be different to meet the needs of these communities, so the research on how to approach them is important."

Nicole's view on the "Initiative's" primary activity is that while it has a business financing focus, its growing strength is in its informal activities, referred to earlier in this book as the psychosocial role.

"We are running more formal and structured mentorship programs and boot camps based on the needs of the participants and changes in the market. But then those connections get formed and the relationships continue. Those relationships don't stop when the formal session is done."

In these, and in Nicole's personal experience, the mentor–mentee relationships become more and more two-way over time.

"The Scotiabank Women Initiative" offers what Nicole calls *"a variety of programming options"* from which the client can choose. Each business line (Business Banking, Global Banking and Markets, and Scotia Wealth Management) has its own team that works online with the Scotiabank branch network that enables the "Initiative" to work with their clients in whatever part of the country they live and work.

There is also industry specialization. There is a lot of engagement in the tech community, for instance, a digital hub to help women accelerate business digitally. They also support women in agriculture with networking events and expertise in succession planning, managing farm risk, and more. Additionally, given the pandemic and its economic impact, there is a lot of work going on in hard-hit business sectors.

In group mentoring sessions, clients have access to senior executives on The Scotiabank Women Initiative Advisory Board. These executives provide expertise to help women grow their businesses. Discussion topics include navigating complex business problems where participants benefit from strengthened relationships and ongoing communication with Scotiabank executives and other women in business.

Feedback and measurement of the effectiveness of the program is regarded as a critical part of the program. Measurement includes:

"The capital deployed; demonstrated success in breaking down the barriers identified by the participants; what feedback we are receiving on the programs and how useful they are; regular full external surveys and how we are being seen in the marketplace in helping women in business."

One of the areas for future development that Nicole envisions is to help women return to work after maternity or other breaks in career: again, an important mentorship role.

Nicole sees the major strengths of the "Initiative" as:

"It is a grassroots program. This has allowed us to be relevant, on the ground, and nimble in terms of what we offer our clients. While the capital is a very important piece, our attendees take advantage of the ecosystem so they can grow through our programs and by participants interacting with each other and their Scotiabank connections."

A significant advantage of "The Scotiabank Women Initiative" is that very connection it creates for an important set of customers and potential customers by listening and serving their needs. It is not only mentorship for women customers but reverse mentoring, as those customers not only help develop each other but also the staff at Scotiabank.

March 25, 2021.

Case #4.3. International Internal Mentorship Programs: IBM

Operating in more than 170 countries globally and No. 38 in revenue in the *Fortune* Global 500 list, IBM is one of the most successful, admired, and long-established names in computing and IT. Its range of services covers cloud computing, AI, commerce data and analytics, Internet of Things, IT infrastructure, mobile and digital workplace, and cyber security.

Interview with Sophie Stanton, Chief Marketing Officer (CMO) IBM Middle East and Africa (MEA). Also, a huge thanks to Mariana Ricardo, IBM MEA Sales & Red Hat Enablement Leader who helped with the background research; and to Miglena Nikolova, Senior Advisory Portfolio Marketing Lead and North American Innovation Lead.

With her most recent move to Dubai to become CMO of IBM Middle East and Africa (MEA), Sophie Stanton has a stellar 15-year career in IBM having worked in marketing, technical support, and sales groups in France and Ireland. Prior to that she had worked in sales in Ireland for Nortel and Gateway following university at the National University of Ireland and school in her native France.

Training and mentorship as part of career development and business success are deeply ingrained in IBM culture. Not only are both widely available and rewarded, they are also a key part of the culture. Sophie Stanton has experienced both extensive and ongoing training and formal and informal mentorship:

"I got a lot out of my mentors over the years and I strongly believe that having mentors really helped me in my career. I have an official mentor on my HR file and I keep in regular contact with that mentor. But I have also had other mentors that I call "heart mentors." People I picked, people who know me well and are able to advise me and challenge me on my thinking or decisions. My "heart mentors" are people I trust will tell me the truth and help me get to the right decisions based on my personality and capability."

While training at IBM is mandatory through its "Think40" program, an expectation of at least 40 hours/year training in technical and increasingly the so-called soft skills, mentorship programs are extensive but not mandatory.

As Sophie comments:

"While there is a world-wide program that gives some guidance on how to get the best out of mentorship, there is no pressure for anyone to have a mentor. It remains very flexible so everyone can find their own way to fit their needs and style."

IBM does offer a myriad of mentorship opportunities and emphasizes its importance. IBM has a long history in providing mentorship to its employees. In 2009, IBM published the book *Intelligent Mentoring: How IBM Creates Value through People, Knowledge and Relationships,* which included techniques and lessons from IBM faculty.

Mentorship programs at IBM are tailored to regional and/or business unit needs and guided by an official "Mentoring Program Framework" which suggests a four-step approach as a guideline for groups setting up mentorship programs:

- Prepare: scope and definition of success, etc.

- Launch: matching of participants, enablement, communications, etc.

- Execute: check-ins, session reports, etc.

- Closing Out: share success, next steps, etc.

As Sophie comments:

"This means they have to think ahead about the program: which mentors and mentees are to be included, what are the goals, how frequently they will meet and so on."

Programs are both global and local and led by different stakeholders (HR, Business Units, Department Leaders, Skills Program Managers, etc.). Guides at IBM have a mentor match algorithm that assists with matches. These can be:

1. Organic Matching: a "low touch" approach recommended for large populations. Mentees search for the program cohort of mentors

based on their titles. They can then filter further by business unit and country. Mentees can review the list of mentors and their profiles, and once a suitable match is found, a compatibility connection should occur.

2. Intelligent Personalized Mentoring: a best practices addition about to be implemented whereby profiles will be enhanced based on interests and skills and based on career paths: IBM Professions, Strategic Technical Skills, Ways of Working Skills, Industry Skills, People Skills, etc.

IBM Mentoring programs support four core components of its global business strategy. The four components are:

- Building organizational intelligence to allow IBM to bridge skill, leadership, and knowledge gaps while creating a climate where collaboration leads to innovation.

- Connecting across people in order to focus on providing support and development across all employee segments.

- Sustaining business impact, which involves integrating mentoring within the overall strategic goals and objectives of the organization.

- Boost minority representation in leadership, improving retention.

Key elements are to:

- Use mentoring to develop tomorrow's world-class business leaders.

- Embrace mentoring as a high-performance work practice.

- Utilize mentoring to strengthen organizational learning, improve retention, promote innovation, and more.

- Use mentoring to serve your organization's most "wicked" problems.

IBM also offers certification for mentors as part of its IBM Professional Program. "IBM Mentor" is a training and mentorship program covering both hard skills and soft skills and requires mentoring a protégé over three months. The badge is awarded *"for developing and cultivating a mentoring relationship with others. Mentoring is an important career development opportunity to enhance skills and achieve long-term career aspirations."* Over 71,000 badges have been awarded to date.

Additionally, many, if not most, training programs at IBM include built-in mentorship connections, programs like the Network Administrator Apprenticeship Certificate, the Technical Solution Seller Apprenticeship, the Application Developer Apprenticeship Certificate and many others.

In terms of marketing mentorships, three examples provide insight into the ongoing thoroughness of IBM's approach.

- The North American Marketing Team in 2019 created a shadowing program called "SidexSide." In 2021, this was extended across the world. The marketing mentees apply to "shadow" an internal senior marketing expert at least two levels above them. They then work together broadening their skills and building new relationships across the marketing disciplines. "SidexSide" has three objectives: (1) build and strengthen relationship networks (2) enable people to experience a day in the life of other roles and disciplines (3) help people identify and learn about potential longer term career paths and skill development areas.

- The second examples are in Canada where several less formal internal and external programs are available. New employees are matched with a mentor to help them adjust to their role and navigate the company. Sometimes these assignments are local and sometimes from the broader North American team. Usually, the mentors are recommended by the mentee's manager or the CMO. Many people approach mentors directly. Canada also launched the "Ten Thousand Coffees mentorship program" in 2020 where people register based on their profile and interest; new interns are paired with experienced IBMers based on common interest. The program introduces the pair but then it is up to each pair how far they will take it. Additionally, external programs like AMA Toronto Mentor Exchange are supported, and a lot of informal mentoring happens within IBM's Business Resource Groups.

- A third example lies in the plans Sophie has for her MEA region in marketing. Her plan will be based on the global programs but also the needs of the local markets, the rapidly changing technology in marketing but also her personal experience:

"When I join a team, I check on my reports to see if they have a mentor and if they think it is the right person. The concept of having the right mentor really depends on what the mentee is looking to get out of the mentoring. Are they looking for hands-on advice on the job if they are new in the role? Or are they looking for something more strategic to help them in their career?

I am building a mentorship program for marketers in the MEA region so that the leaders in my team can mentor the marketers and also benefit from reverse mentoring. It will therefore be a training/mentorship mix of both hard skills and soft skills given the needs in marketing."

Other mentorship programs include the IBM Global Business Services group where a new program for entry level consultants called ELC Mentorship provides opportunities for experienced consultants to share their knowledge while enhancing their own mentorship capabilities. Additionally, in 2020 the "CoachMe" virtual platform was launched for sales personnel. It connects IBM employees across industries, markets and roles. It has more than 600 coaches/mentors lending their time.

In addition to the general mentorship programs, IBM also has programs for specific gender, ethnic and indigenous groups. For example, Sophie recently attended a training/mentoring program of great value to her: "Building Relationships and Influence (BRF)."

"a worldwide program that recognizes that often women don't plan to build relationships in the way that men do. Women tend not to build networks or leverage them as well as men. The program was three days with 20/25 women. First of all, you get to know those people really well, then afterwards there are tools to keep you connected and encourage you to collaborate. For instance, we meet once a quarter and discuss issues. It was super nice to build new connections and learn how to leverage them."

In addition, in 2021 IBM held the "Women's Experience – Express Mentoring Session". Participants connected with two mentors each for a 20-minute session. This was so successful that a call for a series called "Women-Talk@IBM" is continuing. A second example is the "Black, Hispanic, Native American (BHN) Program" where the BHN Mentoring Connect program works specially with diverse groups.

IBM continues to evolve and improve its mentorship approaches. In April 2021, it launched a new global program called "Your Guides at

IBM." This will be a social and collaborative platform to connect IBM employees willing to share expertise with other employees who wish to expand their knowledge. It is a volunteer-based platform where people learn and share their knowledge in an entirely voluntary manner. The platform will allow all employees to search and book a session with a coach or mentor. The search can be classified by Career Paths; IBM Professions; Strategic Technical Skills; Ways of Working Skills (Agile and Design Thinking for example); Industry Skills; People Skills, etc. In addition, there will be newer areas such as developing work-life balance; managing stress; LGBTQ workplace issues, etc. The program will also help the participant use the tool to suggest the best mentor match using AI enabled capabilities to blend criteria like language, skills, profile, etc.

Sophie sees mentorship done properly as a critical tool for good management development. As such in her view, all leaders in an organization should be fully aware of the programs and their value and engaged in them.

"People at any level in an organization can benefit from the right mentor."

She sees the following as key success factors:

- *"It forces you to think long term and to really assess what you expect and need to further your career.*

- *It helps you to stay focused on the milestones to be reached and the deadlines you give yourself.*

- *There is also tremendous value in reverse mentoring for both the people and the organization.*

- *It is a process where the ownership is on the mentee to set up the meetings and the topics: when they want to and when they need to.*

- *It is not the value of a program per se but is the value of reaching out to others for advice: an opportunity to network, better understand other business areas' challenges, and contribute beyond our role.*

- *The main reason mentorship fails is it ends up being passive. They need to be purposeful and a win-win for both the mentee and the mentor. Both need help to get the most from programs. Pairing people and leaving them to their own devices is not enough. People need help on how to make the most of the program(s)."*

Interview: March 29, 2021

5

CONCLUDING THOUGHTS

"I've learned that people will forget what you said, people will forget what you did, but people will never forget how you made them feel."

— Maya Angelou, 1928–2014, American civil rights activist, poet and award-winning author

If we are to achieve a break with traditional industrial era 1.0 organizational thinking and design with all its unnecessary bureaucracy stifling innovation and increasing costs, then the approach outlined in *Humanocracy* is needed. It requires an ever-increasing mentorship approach and one that, while continuing individual mentor–mentee approaches, encompasses more group mentoring and recognition of the work and home life needs of all genders, ages, and ethnic backgrounds.

We have known this for many years.

The COVID-19 pandemic has accelerated many of these changes: most of all the need to fully engage all employees and develop their skills, thinking, and achievement while recognizing and rewarding them. Pyramids of power no longer represent a valid model for optimal organization design. Well-led circles of skills and achievements do. Old concepts of the work-life and the home-life being separate and often competing environments are not helpful or productive. We need to recapture the humanity in all our activities. Let's be remembered for, as Maya Angelou said, for how we make people feel.

Mentorship is a human process. Its roots are deep in human culture. They were too often forgotten through the Industrial Revolution era when the advances of technology often suppressed the humanity. In the new technological age that risk persists. Based on research with U.S. executives conducted between April and November 2020, Gerald Kane et al. discovered the following:

> *"Mentoring and coaching: Employees, particularly younger ones, received less mentoring and coaching during the shift to remote work than they did before the pandemic. If people don't get the feedback they need to develop into more mature employees and leaders, the deficiency could negatively impact career development over time."*

However, some technological breakthroughs enable better treatment and experience. Examples include improved HR systems that enable employee-centred flexibility in managing remote and collocated work, improved digital support for collocated work, improved online communication, continued development of 3D printing, greater use of AI and collaborative robots (cobots) for routine work, and so on.

In this environment, according to *IDC FutureScape: Worldwide Future of Work 2020 Predictions*, by 2024 two-thirds of employees in high-performing companies will shift from static roles to dynamic, outcome-focused reconfigurable teams (much of this was indicated in *Humanocracy*). Organizations will need people, as Sophie Stanton from IBM says:

> *"who can continually learn and adapt. Creating a continuous learning culture does not happen overnight. It goes well beyond having the right technology. To retain and attract top talent in the wake of* COVID*-19, employers need to understand employees' evolving motivations and aspirations."*

A survey done by the IBM Institute for Business Value of 14,000 consumers in nine countries in 2020 indicated that the top two attractions for people about organizations were work-life balance (51%) and career advancement opportunities (43%). Ethics and values were at 41% and continuous learning opportunities were 36%. Compensation was at 41%. The point is that the best people want to be treated as people who can be developed, not just as fixed roles.

The human elements of mentorship are essential to help people work effectively. These should include internal programs to enable people to "onboard" by being introduced to colleagues not only in their immediate work silo but across the organization; external programs that enable learning and development in a broader context than the immediate workplace. And most importantly, the counsel and conversation with people with different experiences and viewpoints.

Mentorship is a way to humanize work relationships and most importantly to encourage all to follow that old adage:

"We have two ears and one mouth so that we can listen twice as much as we speak."

Quote attributed to Epictetus, a Greek philosopher who spent his youth as a slave in Rome before gaining freedom after the death of Nero, under whom he served until around 60 AD.

BIBLIOGRAPHY

"I think that mentoring is such a critical part of the role I play in my position."

— **Michelle Obama, 1964-date, American lawyer, author and former First Lady of the United States**

Adams, Scott. *I Sense a Coldness to Your Mentoring: A Dilbert Book,* Andrews McMeel Publishing, 2013.

Axelrod, W. *10 Steps to Successful Mentoring,* ATD Press, 2019.

Baer, D. "Who's the best person to fast track your career", www.fastcompany.com/3016588 sourced June 16, 2014.

Beakbane, Tom. *How to Understand Everything: Consilience: a new way to see the world,* self –published, 2020.

Bell C. and Goldsmith M. *Managers as Mentors: Building Partnerships for Learning,* BK Publishers Inc., June 2013.

Canada's Top 100 Employers, www.canadastop100.com

de Caraccioli, Louis Antonine. *"The True Mentor or an essay on the education of young people in fashion"* English version, 1760.

Charney, Cy. Lecture Notes from *"Successfully Coaching & Mentoring Individuals & Teams"*, Schulich Executive Education course November 25/26, 2013.

Choudhury, Prithwiraj. *"Our Work-from-Anywhere Future,"* Harvard Business Review November/December 2020, pages 58–67.

Chronus Mentor. *"Start your mentoring program quickly with software from Chronus"* www.chronus.com

Fenelon, Francis. (Francois de Salignec de la Mothe-Fenelon). *"Les Adventures de Telemaque"* 1759.

Ferris, Tim. *Tribe of Mentors*, Houghton Mifflin Harcourt, 2017.

Fisher, C.M, Amabile, T.M. and Pillemer, J. *"How to Help (Without Micromanaging)"* Harvard Business Review, January/February 2021, pages 123–127.

Friedman, Stephen. *"The Essentials of Mentoring Relationships for Mentees"* SEEC/AMA-Toronto Workshop 2020.

Garringer, Michael. *http://www.mentoring.org/senior-leadership-and-staff/$bio-modal-18* and https://www.mentoring.org/virtual-mentoring-portals

Globe and Mail download *"Program connects mentors with young people over a cup of Joe – Ten Thousand Coffees program,"* January 21, 2014.

Graham, Joseph W. *"Mentor: Best Advice in the World"* Columbia, SC29223 pub.2020

Hamel, Gary and Zanini, Michele. *Humanocracy: Creating Organizations as Amazing as the People Inside Them,* Harvard Business Review Press, 2020.

Harvard Business Essentials. *Coaching and Mentoring,* Harvard Business Review Press 2004.

Hawkins P. and Smith N. *Coaching, Mentoring and Organizational Consultancy – Second Edition,* McGraw-Hill Open University Press, 2013.

Hewlett, Sylvia Ann. *Forget a Mentor, Find a Sponsor* Harvard Business School Press 2013.

Ho, Law. *"The Psychology of Coaching, Mentoring and Learning: 2nd Edition",* Wiley and Sons 2013.

Hofestede-insights.com

Homer – translated by Robert Fables. *The Iliad,* Viking Books, 1990.

IBM Institute for Business Value (IBV) survey 2020.

IDC *"FutureScape: Worldwide Future of Work"* October 2020.

IET *"Mentoring Guidelines",* www.iee.org June 28, 2007.

Johnson W.B. and Ridley C.R. *The Elements of Mentoring – 3rd Edition",* St. Martins Press.

Kane, Gerald C.; Phillips, A.; Nanda, R.; A. and Copulsky, J. *"Redesigning the Post-Pandemic Workplace", MIT Sloane Management Review,* February 10, 2021.

Labin, Jenn. *Mentoring Programs that Work,* ATD Press 2017.

Law H. *The Psychology of Coaching, Mentoring and Learning – Second Edition,* Wiley Blackwell, 2013.

Levinson, David; Darrow, Charlotte N.; and Klein, Edward B. *The Seasons of a Man's Life,* Random House, 1978.

LifeMoxie Mentoring. *"Moxie Mentoring"* www.lifemoxie.com 2013.

Mentoring Complete, www.management-mentors.com , 2013.

Mentor: *"International Mentoring Day – Mentoring for a better world"* January 17, 2021 – *"How to Build a Successful Mentoring Program",* National Mentoring Partnership, 2005 www.Mentoring.org

Mitchell, Megan. *"Strength Spotting in Your Mentees"* SEEC/AMA Toronto Workshop 2020.

Murrell, A.J.; Forte-Trammell, D.A.; and Bing, D.A. *Intelligent Mentoring: How IBM Creates Value through People, Knowledge and Relationships.* IBM Press/Pearson plc. 2009.

Poulsen, Kirsten. *"Group mentoring becomes more and more popular"* KMP+/House of Mentoring, kmpplus.com August 24, 2018.

Rhodes, Jean. *The Chronicle of Evidence Based Mentoring,* various editions 2020/2021.

Rolfe, Ann. *Mentoring: Mindset, Skills and Tools – Fourth Edition* Mentoring Works 2020.

Scalia, Vince. *"5 Corporate Mentorship Programs Worth Imitating,"* July 8, 2019 https://blog.gloo.us/corporate-mentorship-program-examples.

Sheehy, Gail. *Passages: Predictable Crises of Adult Life,* 1976.

Triple Creek Associates. *Mentoring Guide for Mentees,* Second Edition 2007.

Triple Creek Associates. *Mentoring Guide for Mentors,* Second Edition 2007.

Urban Land Institute – *"Become a Mentee"* Toronto@uli.org

Via Institute on Character www.viacharacter.org

Vozza, Stephanie. *"Mentor or Best Friend: Which Management Style is Best?"* www.fastcompany.com/3038919, sourced November 27, 2014.

Wilkin, Dave. *"Four Tips for both mentors and mentees"* – speech reported by *The Globe and Mail*, November 27, 2020.

ABOUT THE AUTHOR

"We know what we are, but know not what we may become"

(Hamlet, Act 4, Scene 5, Ophelia)

— William Shakespeare, 1564–1616, English, playwright, poet, actor

Alan C. Middleton's 25-year practitioner career includes marketing roles with the Universal Oil Products Company (UOP Inc.) in Chicago, United States; Esso Petroleum in Oslo, Norway; and a career in advertising with the J. Walter Thompson (JWT) advertising agency in the UK, Canada, and Japan, concluding as President/CEO of JWT Japan and Executive Vice President and a Board Director of the worldwide company.

His 26-year academic career includes teaching at the Rutgers Graduate School of Business in the United States; leading business schools in Argentina, China, India, Russia, and Thailand; and from 1998–2020 he was on the marketing faculty at the Schulich School of Business, York University where he concluded as Distinguished Adjunct Professor of Marketing. From 2001–2020 he was also Executive Director of the Schulich Executive Education Centre (SEEC), which ran non-degree programs for over 10,000 executives and managers a year domestically and internationally. SEEC was continuously ranked in the top 45 executive and management training organizations in the world.

Alan co-authored the books *Advertising Works II, Ikonica – A Fieldguide to Canada's Brandscape,* and has had numerous papers and book chapters published.

He sits on not-for-profit boards and board committees. These include being a founding Advisory Board member of the AMA Toronto Mentor Exchange. He has served continuously since 2010 and has been a mentor every year. He was inducted into the AMA Toronto Canada's Marketing Hall of Legends in the Mentor category in 2005.

He is a co-founder of the Cassie advertising awards, a holder of the ACA Gold Medal for contribution to the marketing industry, the Queen Elizabeth II Diamond Jubilee Medal for service to the literacy movement, and has received the International Association of Business Communicators Toronto Communicator of the Year award.